MAKING CONNECTIONS

INTERMEDIATE

A Strategic Approach to Academic Reading

Teacher's Manual

Jo McEntire
Jessica Williams

CAMBRIDGE
UNIVERSITY PRESS

CAMBRIDGE UNIVERSITY PRESS
Cambridge, New York, Melbourne, Madrid, Cape Town, Singapore, São Paulo, Delhi

Cambridge University Press
32 Avenue of the Americas, New York, NY 10013-2473, USA

www.cambridge.org
Information on this title: www.cambridge.org/9780521730501

First published 2009

Printed in the United States of America

A catalog record for this publication is available from the British Library

ISBN 978-0-521-73049-5 Student's Book
ISBN 978-0-521-73050-1 Teacher's Manual

Cambridge University Press has no responsibility for
the persistence or accuracy of URLs for external or
third-party Internet Web sites referred to in this publication,
and does not guarantee that any content on such
Web sites is, or will remain, accurate or appropriate.

Book design: Adventure House, NYC
Layout services: Page Designs International, Inc.

TABLE OF CONTENTS

TEACHING SUGGESTIONS

The *Making Connections Intermediate* Student's Book consists of six units, each of which is organized in the following way:

- Two **Skills and Strategies** sections alternate with the Readings. The first precedes Readings 1 and 2, and the second precedes Readings 3 and 4. These sections introduce and practice specific skills and strategies for reading. For easier orientation and reference, all Skills and Strategies pages are orange.
- **Four readings** are each accompanied by associated activities in pre-reading, reading, vocabulary building and review, research, discussion, and writing. Readings 1–3 have an average length of 7 paragraphs. Reading 4 has an average length of 11 paragraphs, and offers students a reading experience closer to the challenges of the reading assignments they will meet in their future academic studies.
- A final section, **Making Connections**, provides coherence-building tasks and a review of the vocabulary introduced in the unit.

Intermediate-level students need to expand their vocabulary in order to prepare for academic courses. Strategies and activities to help students expand their vocabulary are therefore important features of *Making Connections Intermediate*. The first Skills and Strategies section in each unit focuses on techniques for vocabulary building. The post-reading activities following each of the four readings in a unit include tasks that facilitate vocabulary expansion by focusing on 15 to 20 vocabulary items used in the reading. These vocabulary items are listed and defined, with an example provided, in Appendix 1 of the Student's Book (pages 243–261). In Appendix 2 of the Student's Book (pages 262–264), each key vocabulary item is indexed by the reading in which it is first used.

Making Connections Intermediate has enough material for a reading course of 50 to 70 class hours, assuming a corresponding number of hours are available for homework assignments. Completing all the Beyond the Reading tasks that accompany each reading might make the course longer.

Skills, strategies, and vocabulary are recycled within a unit and in subsequent units. It is recommended, therefore, that in planning a course outline, the order of the book be followed.

SKILLS AND STRATEGIES

The Skills and Strategies sections are printed on orange pages so that they are easily distinguishable and readily located. These sections introduce text features and associated reading strategies that are then incorporated into the reading activities.

Rationale

Research suggests that good readers apply various strategies when they are reading a text. The Skills and Strategies sections introduce and provide practice with a variety of these reading strategies.

Description

The first Skills and Strategies section of each unit introduces vocabulary-building skills and strategies: understanding vocabulary in context, using the dictionary, the vocabulary of numbers, increasing reading speed, vocabulary study, and collocation. The second Skills and Strategies section in each unit focuses on reading strategies: finding main ideas and supporting details, understanding graphical information, scanning, taking notes, and preparing for a reading test.

Each Skills and Strategies section provides three Skill Practice tasks that move students from recognition to production. Further practice is provided in the While You Read section. Once introduced, strategies are recycled throughout the text.

How to Use

The Skills and Strategies sections are best introduced in class, supported by the use of other materials (e.g., overheads of examples similar to those in the "Examples and Explanations" subsection). At the beginning of the course, each of the Skill Practice tasks should be partially completed in class. Then, when you are confident that your students understand the form and content of each exercise, an appropriate number of items can be assigned for homework.

READINGS

In each unit of *Making Connections Intermediate*, there are three shorter readings and one longer reading. The tasks that accompany the readings are described below, together with their rationale and some notes on how to use the tasks effectively in the classroom.

GETTING INTO THE TOPIC

Rationale

The purpose of this task is to get students to activate background knowledge relevant to the content of the reading that follows. Effective reading occurs when readers are able to place new information within the context of information they already possess.

Description

This is the first of two pre-reading activities that occur before each article. It consists of questions for discussion with a partner.

How to Use

This activity can be introduced through short, full-class discussions. The discussions can then be continued by partners or groups of three.

GETTING A FIRST IDEA ABOUT THE ARTICLE

Rationale

The purpose of this task is to get students into the habit of previewing the content and organization of a text before they start reading in depth. Previewing has been shown to be a key strategy that enhances a reader's ability to understand a text on first encounter.

Description

Making Connections Intermediate uses different techniques for previewing texts. Students are taught to look at titles, headings, pictures, and graphic information such as charts to guess what information might appear, or to form questions that they expect the article to answer. Another technique has the student matching questions and topics to paragraphs. Each technique encourages the student to interact with the text before beginning to read for deeper understanding.

How to Use

These activities are best introduced, modeled, and practiced in class. We recommend that students first work with a partner as they complete this task. The primary goal of this activity is to encourage active interaction with the text. Student answers may vary from those provided in the Answer Key, but it is the discussion about these answers that is more important than the answers themselves. Please feel free to supplement with other strategies that strike you as useful for previewing a given reading. Later, as your students become comfortable working with less guidance, these activities may be completed individually or as homework assignments.

WHILE YOU READ

Rationale

Research suggests that good readers read actively by asking themselves questions and monitoring comprehension as they read. The While You Read tasks encourage students to adopt this approach. These tasks focus students' attention on the strategic nature of the reading process during their first read-through of a text. These tasks appear in the margins of the text and force students to stop and apply the strategies presented in the earlier Skills and Strategies sections. Students are thus encouraged to do what good readers do – to interact with the text while they read.

Description

While You Read boxes are in orange in the margin of every reading, opposite some boldface words within a line of text. Students are directed to stop reading at the end of the sentence containing the boldface text and to perform a strategic task designed to support effective reading.

While You Read provides practice for the skills and strategies introduced in the preceding Skills and Strategies section as well as those introduced in earlier units. It reinforces lexical skills by having students identify context clues to meaning, figure out a word's part of speech, look up challenging words in a dictionary, and recognize collocations. It provides practice in reading skills by having students identify main ideas and supporting details, understand connections between paragraphs, annotate while reading, and outline paragraphs.

Students demonstrate their understanding of these strategies in various ways: highlighting stretches of text, underlining or circling shorter text elements, drawing simple diagrams, making notes in the margin, or choosing an answer to a question.

How to Use

While You Read is best introduced and modeled as a classroom activity after the text has been previewed. We recommend that you first introduce students to the concept of active reading. You can do this by reading the first article of Unit 1 out loud. As you come to each boldface word, stop and read the While You Read directions. Answer the question before you continue to read. Note that this technique will be new to many students, particularly those who do not read extensively in their own language. Students will find it a time-consuming process at first, but assure them that, with practice, they will gradually apply these strategies automatically and their reading speed and comprehension will increase.

At first, many, or perhaps all, of the boxes in the shorter readings can be completed during an initial in-class read-through. This will allow you to provide students with the intensive guidance, practice, and immediate feedback on their performances that they will need as they learn to apply these skills independently.

To help students focus on the reading process, it is strongly recommended that no dictionary be used during this first read-through. We also recommend that the first read-through includes reading for main ideas. (See the Main Idea Check section below.)

During the first few weeks of using *Making Connections Intermediate*, as students become accustomed to incorporating conscious strategy-use into their reading, it is important that teachers offer support by monitoring and providing clear and timely feedback on student responses to the While You Read tasks. These tasks require students to mark up their texts in ways that will be easily visible as you move around the classroom. This "real-time" checking provides you with valuable feedback on how successfully your students are applying a suggested reading strategy and enables you to suggest some "real-time" solutions if they are having difficulty. Your suggestions can be reinforced if you provide students with short answer keys for the While You Read boxes, which they can use to make adjustments as they continue reading the article for homework.

There may be other strategies that you think would be useful for your students' first read-through of a given article. As a way to gain your own insights into strategies that are appropriate, we recommend that you first read the articles in *Making Connections Intermediate* as you would read any articles for your own interest and information, rather than as texts you are going to teach. This will give you the opportunity to observe your own strategies in action and to identify some you might wish to add to those presented in *Making Connections Intermediate*.

The principle danger in the While You Read activity is that some students make excessive use of highlighting and/or underlining. Try to help students understand that highlighting or underlining entire paragraphs, for example, is not an effective reading strategy. In fact, indiscriminate highlighting is a counterproductive activity. To avoid this, have the students follow the directions provided in the Skills and Strategies sections: circle main ideas, number supporting details, and highlight only key vocabulary.

MAIN IDEA CHECK

Rationale

Students often focus too much on the details in a text rather than on its main ideas. The Main Idea Check tasks provide an opportunity for students to focus on an understanding of the main ideas of each paragraph. It is only after students have grasped the main ideas of a text that they can make sense of how the details fit into this larger frame of meaning.

Description

For the first two readings of Unit 1, the Main Idea Check asks students to choose from four options the sentence that best expresses the main idea of the entire article. For the remainder of the readings, the Main Idea Check has students identify the main idea of each paragraph by matching the paragraph number to the sentence expressing its main idea.

How to Use

Before starting the Main Idea Check tasks in Unit 1, we recommend that you read Skills and Strategies 2 in Unit 1 so that you know the main idea identification strategies that will be explicitly introduced there.

For Unit 1 Readings 1 and 2, use a simple approach with which you are comfortable, without going into the issue in any great detail. It would be helpful, for example, to have students discuss why the other choices do not represent the main idea of the reading.

We recommend that students identify the main idea immediately after finishing each paragraph for two reasons. First, the content of the paragraph is still fresh in their minds. Second, this timing better approximates the timing of main idea decisions in real reading. Students may question this approach, as it interrupts the fluency of their reading. You may need to explain the difference between reading for pleasure (which should be fluent and free from interruption) and reading academic texts, which requires constant checking and rereading for comprehension. Once the students have read through the article identifying main ideas, they should reread it. This second reading will be more fluent.

We also recommend making completion of the While You Read and Main Idea Check the goal of the first read-through of each reading. To help students focus on these activities, dictionaries should not be used during this first read-through. Skills and Strategies 1 in Unit 1 provides instruction and practice in dealing with unknown vocabulary. We also recommend in-class completion of the first read-throughs of at least Unit 1 in order to show students that this dictionary-free approach to a text, though initially often new and unsettling for them, is both feasible and helpful.

After you work through the strategy-based approach to main idea identification in Skills and Strategies 2, Unit 1, the Main Idea Check tasks may be assigned for work in class or for homework. In classes with additional writing goals, students could be asked to rewrite the sentences of the Main Idea Check tasks in their own words and then put the sentences together to form a summary of the given article or passage.

A CLOSER LOOK

Rationale

Having understood the main ideas in a text, students need to achieve a more in-depth understanding of the text. In these tasks, therefore, students are asked to go back to the text and read for details and to establish connections among them.

Description

Many of the questions in A Closer Look are types of questions with which students will probably be familiar (e.g., true/false and multiple choice). We recommend that early on in the text, perhaps in Unit 2, you review some common strategies in answering multiple-choice questions. You can encourage students to use the following strategies:

- Read the directions very carefully.
- Read all the possible answers before choosing the correct one.
- Eliminate the obviously incorrect answers.
- Recognize that a wrong answer may include an incorrect fact or information not in the article.
- Recognize that all information within the answer must be true for the answer to be correct.

You should also alert students to one question type that is possibly less familiar. To encourage the synthesizing of information, a significant number of multiple-choice questions have more than one correct answer. This question type is introduced by the directions *Circle all that apply*.

How to Use

Generally, the activities in A Closer Look lend themselves well to completion outside of class. However, we suggest that at first you give students some classroom practice in answering this section.

Appendix 1, Key Vocabulary from the Readings (pages 243–261 in the Student's Book), is a useful tool for students as they complete A Closer Look activities. This appendix lists the vocabulary alphabetically within each reading, thus providing accessible and convenient support for students during these more detailed examinations of articles. For more information on Appendix 1, see page 9.

VOCABULARY STUDY: SYNONYMS

Rationale

These tasks provide a simple and structured way for students to take their first steps in learning the target vocabulary in each of the 24 readings.

Description

The Synonyms exercise follows A Closer Look after each reading. In this activity, students find a word in the article that is similar in meaning to each of 10 given definitions. This is a simple way for students to focus on target vocabulary in context without having to use bilingual dictionaries. Part-of-speech information about the target vocabulary has been provided so that students can integrate this information into the vocabulary-learning process.

How to Use

This activity is best introduced as a classroom activity. It can then be completed either in or out of class as homework.

VOCABULARY STUDY: WORDS IN CONTEXT

Rationale

Understanding the meaning of unknown target words by perceiving the surrounding context of the word has been demonstrated to be a vital skill in vocabulary acquisition. This task helps students to see the linguistic contexts in which the target words belong.

Description

The Words in Context exercise is introduced after the first and third readings of each unit. This is a fill-in-the-blank task with 10 words or phrases from the reading that have not been targeted in the preceding Synonyms exercise. The key vocabulary items are presented in the orange box at the beginning of the activity.

How to Use

This task can be completed either in or out of class. Encourage students to go back to the text and find the target words if they cannot readily answer the questions. Although these words are recycled in later readings, we encourage you to expand this practice by creating vocabulary tests focusing on these target words. Testing students on some of the vocabulary from Unit 1 while they are working on later units, for example, will help them to retain vocabulary.

VOCABULARY STUDY: WORD FAMILIES

Rationale

Intermediate-level learners need to build their academic vocabulary quickly in order to be successful in more advanced courses. Recognizing different word forms allows students to increase their receptive vocabulary quickly and efficiently. By focusing on parts of speech, this approach to vocabulary building also may help students move toward the ability to use the vocabulary in writing and speech.

Description

This exercise is introduced after the Synonyms exercise in the second and fourth readings of each unit. It introduces five word families. Each exercise contains the common noun and verb form of the target word, and either the adjective or adverb form (if applicable). The boldface word in each family is the part of speech that appears in the reading. Students are instructed to locate the words in the reading and use context clues to figure out the meanings. If the students are still unsure, you may direct them to Appendix 1 to check the meaning of unfamiliar vocabulary. Two forms of each of the five word families are used to complete the 10 fill-in-the-blank sentences.

How to Use

We recommend that you introduce this activity in class, as students may need more instruction in parts of speech. They may also need guidance in using the correct form of the word.

VOCABULARY REVIEW: SAME OR DIFFERENT

Rationale

This task performs several important functions. It provides further opportunities for students to work with the vocabulary they have already encountered; it develops their skill for recognizing paraphrases; and it helps move students away from a "word-centered" approach to reading.

Description

Same or Different tasks follow Word Families after Readings 2 and 4 of each unit. Same or Different tasks consist of six pairs of sentences incorporating vocabulary items introduced in Readings 1 and 2 and in Readings 3 and 4 of a given unit. Students are asked to decide on the semantic equivalence of the two sentences in each pair.

How to Use

Same or Different is best completed in class until students become comfortable with its requirements. As students work in class, it would be a good idea for you to ask questions that focus their attention on the meaning of the sentence in the left-hand column and elements of the sentence in the right-hand column that make that sentence similar or different in meaning.

BEYOND THE READING

Rationale

Some teachers may want to use the texts as an opportunity for their students to do further discussion, undertake some research on the topic of the reading, and/or do some writing. This final section of the post-reading tasks provides such an opportunity.

Description

This activity occurs after each of the 24 readings. It offers topics for students to research and discuss that are relevant to the subject of the article they have just read. A short writing assignment, usually based on the results of their research or discussion, is provided as the final component of this activity.

How to Use

The research questions offer opportunities for students to tackle more challenging reading tasks as well as to pursue more personally stimulating aspects of a given topic. Some of the research requires students to do self-reflection or survey classmates to gather more data. Some requires students to go to the Web to find additional information. Discussion activities offer students the opportunity to combine their own ideas with knowledge gained from the reading. As a follow-up activity, the writing assignment will allow students to use their discussions and/or research findings as the basis to write one or two short paragraphs, which can be produced either in or outside of class.

MAKING CONNECTIONS

As the final review activities of each unit, these two tasks give students practice in establishing within short texts the coherence of vocabulary, structural features, and organizational patterns.

Rationale

These tasks provide students with a focused opportunity to practice reading for coherence between sentences and short paragraphs. In addition, students get a further opportunity to review recently-targeted academic vocabulary.

Description

Units 1 to 4 introduce and give students practice with strategies writers use to achieve coherence:

- Repetition of key words or phrases
- Use of pronouns and antecedents
- Use of cause-and-effect transition words
- Use of contrast transition words

Units 5 and 6 allow students to review and apply all four strategies.

Each Making Connections section consists of two exercises. The first exercise directs students to identify coherence strategies within one or two sentences. They do this by underlining, highlighting, or drawing arrows from one part of the text to another.

The second exercise expands practice to the paragraph level. Each item consists of a lead sentence followed by three sentences labeled A, B, and C. Students are asked to decide the order of these three sentences to produce a coherent short paragraph. Item topics are similar to the topics in the readings of the unit, thus refamiliarizing students with the key vocabulary items from the unit.

How to Use

This activity is probably best performed in class, where fairly immediate feedback is available. Students can work individually or in pairs. Feedback may be supplied by you and/or elicited from students. You can expand this practice by presenting other jigsaw-type activities. For example, take a paragraph that uses the same coherence-building strategies. Enlarge it and cut and paste individual sentences onto note cards or an overhead. Have the students practice putting the paragraph back into order by using the strategies they have learned.

APPENDICES

APPENDIX 1: KEY VOCABULARY FROM THE READINGS (pages 243–261)

Appendix 1 is the "dictionary" for *Making Connections Intermediate*. For each reading, the target vocabulary items are listed alphabetically, defined simply and clearly, and exemplified in a sentence. The dictionary's purpose is to offer students easy access to information on the meaning and use of each word during the vocabulary learning process, especially while they are completing the Vocabulary Study and Vocabulary Review activities. It can also be used during students' work on A Closer Look.

APPENDIX 2: INDEX TO KEY VOCABULARY (pages 262–264)

This index lists each key vocabulary item by the reading in which it is first introduced, thus allowing students to locate the original dictionary entry for a vocabulary item when necessary (e.g., when a student wishes to review a word after seeing it again in a subsequent reading).

ANSWER KEY

 **The News Media**

SKILLS AND STRATEGIES 1 UNDERSTANDING VOCABULARY IN CONTEXT

SKILL PRACTICE 1 (pages 3–4)

Answers will vary.

2	b	For instance
3	c	In contrast
4	b, d	such as
5	b	
6	a	
7	b	for example
8	d	
9	a, b, d	such as
10	d	

SKILL PRACTICE 2 (pages 4–5)

2 b **3** c **4** b **5** c **6** a **7** d **8** c **9** d **10** c

SKILL PRACTICE 3 (page 6)

Answers will vary.
2 different from the usual
3 providing lots of useful information
4 people who buy goods or services
5 very shocking
6 stop from doing something that you want to do
7 hopeful and confident, or giving cause for hope and confidence
8 get back something lost, especially health

READING 1 THE NEWS MEDIA IN THE PAST

GETTING A FIRST IDEA ABOUT THE ARTICLE (page 7)

1 the history of news media
2 a, d

WHILE YOU READ (pages 8–9)
by word of mouth
  spreading news by talking to people (Par. 1, lines 6–8)

illiterate

This meant that (Par. 2, lines 7–8)

life in Europe and North America was changing

(1) New industries needed more educated workers . . . more schools.

(2) As a result, more people learned to read.

(3) In addition, new technology . . . newspapers were much cheaper.

(4) Finally, . . . large numbers of immigrants were arriving. (Par. 4, lines 1–7)

cables

(or) large wires (Par. 5, line 5)

MAIN IDEA CHECK (page 9)

Choice d is correct.

Choice a is too general.

Choice b is one detail.

Choice c is not covered in the article.

A CLOSER LOOK (pages 9–10)

1 False (Par. 1, lines 1–5)

2 d (Par. 2, lines 3–7)

3 c (Par. 3, lines 9–11)

4 a (Par. 4, lines 4–6); b (Par. 4, lines 9–10); c (Par. 4, lines 7–8, 10–12); d (Par. 4, line 4)

5 False (Par. 5, lines 9–10)

6 1400s – invention of the printing press; printed news came out in one-page reports (Par. 3, lines 1–3)

1690 – first American newspaper started in Boston (Par. 3, lines 7–8)

1752 – first Canadian newspaper started (Par. 3, line 8)

1840s – technology improved; industry expanded; more people learned to read, newspapers increased in popularity (Par. 4)

1860s – cables were built under the oceans; news could travel very quickly (Par. 5, lines 5–7)

1883 – Krakatoa erupted; news was reported same day (Par. 5, lines 7–12)

VOCABULARY STUDY: SYNONYMS (page 10)

1 local **2** villagers **3** gather(ed) **4** crimes **5** afford **6** reduce(d) **7** eager **8** wires **9** instantly **10** cables

VOCABULARY STUDY: WORDS IN CONTEXT (page 11)

1 focused on **2** natural disasters **3** entertaining **4** publish **5** erupt **6** average **7** by word of mouth **8** popular **9** appetite **10** dramatically

READING 2 THE HISTORY OF ELECTRONIC MEDIA

GETTING A FIRST IDEA ABOUT THE ARTICLE (page 13)

A 3 **B** 2 **C** 1 **D** 5 **E** 4

WHILE YOU READ (pages 14–15)

live events

at the same time as they were happening (Par. 1, line 6)

(1) cricket match (Par. 1, lines 7–8)

(2) World War II (Par. 1, lines 10–11)

accessible

easily gotten (Par. 2, lines 5–7)

this negative news
Every night on the news . . . watched American soldiers and Vietnamese citizens die. (Par. 3, lines 7–8)

around the clock
Twenty-four hours a day (Par. 4, line 5)

digital media
electronic media such as the Internet, cell phones, and MP3 players (Par. 5, lines 6–7)

MAIN IDEA CHECK (page 16)

Choice d is correct.
Choice a is not true and does not include the Internet.
Choice b is one specific detail.
Choice c is too general and does not include information about the Internet.

A CLOSER LOOK (page 16)

1 a (Par. 1, lines 4–5); c (Par. 1, lines 5–7); d (Par. 1, line 11)
2 True (Par. 2)
3 c (Par. 3, lines 3–4)
4 b (Par. 4, lines 2–3)
5 False (Par. 4, lines 10–11)
6

TRADITIONAL	DIGITAL
newspapers (Par. 5, line 2)	computers (Par. 5, line 6)
television (Par. 5, line 2)	cell phones (Par. 5, line 7)
	MP3 players (Par. 5, line 7)

VOCABULARY STUDY: SYNONYMS (page 17)

1 transmit 2 live 3 convenient 4 batteries 5 (to) broadcast 6 global 7 impact 8 frequently
9 available 10 pace

VOCABULARY STUDY: WORD FAMILIES (pages 17–18)

1 access 2 influential 3 traditions 4 acceleration 5 traditional 6 influence 7 significant 8 access
9 accelerate 10 significance

VOCABULARY REVIEW: SAME OR DIFFERENT (page 18)

1 D 2 D 3 S 4 D 5 D 6 S

SKILLS AND STRATEGIES 2 FINDING MAIN IDEAS

SKILL PRACTICE 1 (pages 21–22)

1 a 2 a 3 c 4 b

SKILL PRACTICE 2 (page 22)

1 b 2 d 3 a 4 b

SKILL PRACTICE 3 (page 23)

1 c
2 d
3 Pulitzer wanted journalism to be a respected profession.

READING 3 CITIZEN JOURNALISM

GETTING A FIRST IDEA ABOUT THE ARTICLE (page 24)

A 2 **B** 4 **C** 1 **D** 7 **E** 6 **F** 5 **G** 3

WHILE YOU READ (pages 25–26)

or *bloggers*

Topic: (The news media today)

Claim: is in one of the most significant periods of change in its history. (Par. 1, lines 1–2)

In most cases, reporters and editors decided what was news and what was not news.

This sentence (a) restates the main idea. (Par. 2)

posting

adding (Par. 3, line 7)

the disaster

The second sentence contains the main idea: (Citizen journalists have the same technology as traditional reporters and can easily publish news.) (Par. 3, lines 2–3)

every citizen can be a reporter

Topic: (OhmyNews Web site)

Claim: publishes hundreds of stories every day. (Par. 4, lines 1–3)

These examples

(1) In 2002, a United States senator, Trent Lott, made racist statements. . . . Finally, the senator had to resign from his position. (Par. 5, lines 2–8)

(2) Another famous person to lose his job because of bloggers was Dan Rather, an American television journalist. . . . Rather also had to resign from his job. (Par. 5, lines 8–13)

do business

(Online news sites) (Par. 7, line 1)

MAIN IDEA CHECK (page 27)

Paragraphs 1–4

A 2 **B** 4 **C** 1 **D** 3

Paragraphs 5–7

E 7 **F** 5 **G** 6

A CLOSER LOOK (pages 27–28)

1 False (Par. 1, lines 6–7)
2 A *blog* is an online journal. (Par. 3, lines 4–5)
3 True (Par. 3)
4 d (Par. 4, lines 7–9)
5 b (Par. 5, lines 8–14)
6 a (Par. 3, lines 13–15); c (Par. 6, lines 6–7); d (Par. 3, lines 9–11)
7 True (Par. 6, lines 1–2)
8 a (Par. 7, lines 2–4)

VOCABULARY STUDY: SYNONYMS (page 28)

1 cheap **2** transform(ed) **3** research(ed) **4** editors **5** devastation **6** survivors **7** (to) resign
8 inaccurate **9** absolute **10** solution

VOCABULARY STUDY: WORDS IN CONTEXT (page 29)

1 concept **2** founded **3** execution **4** racist **5** advertising **6** rejected **7** audience **8** inferior to
9 control **10** well-trained

READING 4 ETHICAL REPORTING

GETTING A FIRST IDEA ABOUT THE ARTICLE (page 30)

PARAGRAPH	TOPIC
2	Reporters going undercover
4	Reporting illegal activities
5	Reporters breaking the law
6	Reporting the truth
8	The paparazzi
9	Selling the news

WHILE YOU READ (pages 31–33)

tempt
to encourage someone to do something – especially something wrong (Par. 1, lines 1–3)

going undercover
pretending to be someone else in order to find out information (Par. 2, lines 1–4)

many examples
(1) Ryan Parry (Par. 3, line 2)
(2) a journalist . . . at London's Heathrow Airport (Par. 3, lines 5–6)
(3) In South Korea, reporters went undercover (Par. 4, lines 2–3)
(4) In the United States, a group of television reporters (Par. 4, lines 6–7)

meat and fish department
Reporters go undercover to report on health and food safety. (Par. 4)

journalists must always tell the truth
Can they lie? (Par. 1, line 6)

but the public wants to read about it
Topic: The public has a huge appetite for news about the rich and famous
Claim: so reporters are under pressure to write stories about these celebrities (Par. 7, lines 2–4)

sensational
very exciting (Par. 9)

MAIN IDEA CHECK (page 33)

Paragraphs 1–5
A 3 **B** 2 **C** 1 **D** 5 **E** 4
Paragraphs 6–9
F 6 **G** 9 **H** 8 **I** 7

A CLOSER LOOK (pages 34–35)

1 a, b (Par. 3, lines 1–5)

2

UNDERCOVER REPORTER	RESULT
Nellie Bly	Changes were made in how people were treated in mental hospitals. (Par. 2, lines 10–12)
Ryan Parry	Security at Buckingham Palace was improved. (Par. 5, lines 5–6)
A journalist at Heathrow Airport	Security at Heathrow Airport was improved. (Par. 5, lines 5–6)
South Korean journalists	New laws against throwing poisonous chemicals into the sea were created. (Par. 5, lines 6–8)
Television reporters at a U.S. supermarket	Health improvements were made in the meat and fish departments. (Par. 4, lines 11–13)

3 a (Par. 2, lines 3–5; Par. 3, lines 1–2)   **4** True (Par. 5, lines 1–2)   **5** True (Par. 5, lines 10–12)

6 (1) Cooke wanted to write a sensational news story. (Par. 6, lines 3–6)
(2) Cooke wrote a story about a young boy who lived in a world of drugs. (Par. 6, lines 4–6)
(3) People all over the United States read Cooke's story. (Par. 6, line 7)
(4) Cooke won a Pulitzer Prize. (Par. 6, lines 9–10)
(5) Cooke finally told everyone that her story was not true. (Par. 6, lines 11–12)
(6) The newspaper returned Cooke's Pulitzer Prize. (Par. 6, lines 12–13)

7 True (Par. 7, lines 7–8)   **8** b (Par. 8, lines 10–14)

VOCABULARY STUDY: SYNONYMS (page 35)

1 pressure   **2** pretend   **3** mentally ill   **4** security   **5** fake   **6** documents   **7** illegal   **8** shocked   **9** addict
10 celebrities

VOCABULARY STUDY: WORD FAMILIES (page 36)

1 complaints   **2** poisonous   **3** privacy   **4** confessed   **5** beneficial   **6** complained   **7** private   **8** poison
9 benefits   **10** confession

VOCABULARY REVIEW: SAME OR DIFFERENT (page 37)

1 D   **2** D   **3** S   **4** D   **5** S   **6** S

MAKING CONNECTIONS

EXERCISE 1 (pages 38–39)

2 blogs – Popular blogs; Popular – The most popular; Boing Boing – it

3 July 20th, 1969 – That day; watched – watched; people all over the world – international audience

4 Journalists – Journalists; a president or prime minister – the American President, Richard Nixon; a newspaper report written by two journalists – Their story

5 bureaus – these news bureaus; international – all over the world; smaller newspapers – these smaller companies

EXERCISE 2 (pages 39–40)

1 B, A, C
2 C, A, B
3 C, A, B
4 C, A, B
5 C, B, A

UNIT 2 Education

SKILLS AND STRATEGIES 3 USING THE DICTIONARY

SKILL PRACTICE 1 (pages 43–44)

1 students; high scores b
2 university b
3 national university a
4 metric system; most of the world a
5 religious organizations; schools b

SKILL PRACTICE 2 (pages 44–45)

1 b **2** b **3** a **4** b **5** a

SKILL PRACTICE 3 (page 45)

2 find a similarity or connection between two things
3 left someone or something in a difficult situation
4 right or just
5 usual or frequent
6 changed
7 learn
8 very important
9 very sure
10 not strong; slight

READING 1 EDUCATION AROUND THE WORLD

GETTING A FIRST IDEA ABOUT THE ARTICLE (page 46)

Answers will vary.

	POSSIBLE CONTENT OF THE ARTICLE
TITLE	Description of education in different countries
PHOTO	Different types of classrooms; different ways of teaching
GRAPH	The economic benefits of education

WHILE YOU READ (pages 47–49)

elite
   poor and uneducated people (Par. 1)

moral instruction
   moral instruction (*n*) teaching children about how to behave in a good and honest way (Par. 2, line 6)

challenge
   Challenge is a noun in this sentence. Students should underline <u>a</u>. (Par. 5, line 1); something that requires an effort to be done successfully (Par. 5)

part of mosques
   Most students attend government schools, but some students attend private ones. (Par. 6, lines 7–8)

individuals

Individuals is a noun in this sentence. Students should underline <u>individuals</u>, <u>nations</u>. (Par. 7, line 1)

MAIN IDEA CHECK (pages 49–50)

Paragraphs 1–4
A 2 **B** 3 **C** 1 **D** 4

Paragraphs 5–7
E 7 **F** 6 **G** 5

A CLOSER LOOK (page 50)

1 b (Par. 1, lines 8–9); d (Par. 1, lines 7–8)
2 a (Par. 2, lines 12–13)
3 c (Par. 4)
4 True (Par. 6, line 7)
5 (1) They believe private schools offer a better education than government schools. (Par. 6, lines 9–10)
   (2) Some parents do not agree with the curriculum in government schools. (Par. 6, lines 11–12)
6 c (Par. 7, Figure 2.1)

VOCABULARY STUDY: SYNONYMS (page 51)

1 development **2** compulsory **3** advantage **4** emphasize **5** opportunity **6** elsewhere **7** compromise
8 fees **9** taxes **10** productivity

VOCABULARY STUDY: WORDS IN CONTEXT (page 51)

1 industrialization **2** individuals **3** meet the need **4** expanded **5** moral instruction **6** contributed to
7 funding **8** curriculum **9** academic **10** take care of

READING 2 TESTING IN EDUCATION

GETTING A FIRST IDEA ABOUT THE ARTICLE (page 53)

A 3 **B** 6 **C** 5 **D** 4 **E** 1 **F** 2

WHILE YOU READ (pages 54–56)

people's lives
   Topic: (tests) (Par. 1, line 5)
   Claim: <u>They are a regular part of education, and they often have a significant impact on people's lives.</u>
   (Par. 1, lines 5–7)

standardized tests
   Students can use lines 9–11 in Par. 1 as context clues; tests written by testing professionals that are
   given to large groups of people

colonies
   <u>India</u>, <u>Tanzania</u>, and <u>Malaysia</u> (Par. 3, lines 3–4)

admission
   (a) a noun; **admission** (*n*) entry

sign autographs
   In this sentence, *sign* is a verb that the subject *they* (teachers) performs. The correct definition of *sign*
   in *sign autographs* is when people, usually celebrities, write their names. (Par. 5, lines 14–16)

MAIN IDEA CHECK (page 56)

A 5 **B** 3 **C** 6 **D** 4 **E** 1 **F** 2

A CLOSER LOOK (pages 56–57)

1 False (Par. 1, lines 10–11)
2 b (Par. 2, line 3); c (Par. 2, lines 6–8)
3 b (Par. 2, lines 10–12)
4 b, d (Par. 4)
5 a (Par. 4, lines 9–10); b (Par. 5, lines 4–6); d (Par. 5, lines 2–4)
6 an extra $10,000 a year (Par. 5, lines 2–4)
7 True (Par. 6, lines 7–9, Table 2.1)

VOCABULARY STUDY: SYNONYMS (page 57)

1 colonies **2** factors **3** consider **4** enormous **5** cheating **6** obtain(ed) **7** profit **8** superstars
9 autographs **10** policies

VOCABULARY STUDY: WORD FAMILIES (page 58)

1 separate **2** competition **3** performance **4** evaluation **5** efficiency **6** evaluated **7** perform
8 separate **9** efficient **10** competed

VOCABULARY REVIEW: SAME OR DIFFERENT (page 59)

1 D **2** S **3** D **4** S **5** S **6** D

SKILLS AND STRATEGIES 4 FINDING SUPPORTING DETAILS

SKILL PRACTICE 1 (page 61)

1 A S; **B** M **2 A** M; **B** S **3 A** S; **B** M **4 A** M; **B** S **5 A** M; **B** S

SKILL PRACTICE 2 (page 62)

1 A S; **B** M; **C** S **2 A** S; **B** M; **C** S **3 A** S; **B** S; **C** M **4 A** S; **B** S; **C** M **5 A** M; **B** S; **C** S

SKILL PRACTICE 3 (pages 62–63)

1 Supporting detail: First, the teacher had to learn how to teach with no training.
Supporting detail: The teacher was . . . sometimes as young as sixteen years old.
Supporting detail: She had to . . . and sweep the floors. She often cooked breakfast . . .
Supporting detail: Then she had to teach all subjects to children of all ages.
2 Supporting detail: . . . immigrants have always had to learn English . . .
Supporting detail: . . . easiest way to speak English is to speak it in all classes.
Supporting detail: . . . it will be harder for children if they speak two languages. . . .
3 Supporting detail: On the first day, teachers gave the children new English names . . .
Supporting detail: . . . and cut their long hair.
Supporting detail: The children were permitted to speak only English . . .
Supporting detail: . . . did not allow them to practice their own religion.

READING 3 ALTERNATIVE EDUCATION

GETTING A FIRST IDEA ABOUT THE ARTICLE (page 64)

A 3 **B** 4 **C** 1 **D** 2 **E** 7 **F** 8 **G** 6 **H** 5

WHILE YOU READ (pages 65–67)

obsolete
no longer useful (Par. 1, lines 7–10)

demand
Demand is (a) a noun in this sentence; the need for something (Par. 3, lines 4–6)

reasons
Supporting details:
(1) Some disagree with standardized tests and do not like a traditional curriculum. (Par. 4, lines 4–5)
(2) Others choose to homeschool because they want to emphasize religious and moral instruction. (Par. 4, lines 5–6)
(3) Many parents also see homeschooling as an opportunity to spend more time with their children. (Par. 4, lines 6–8)

learners
The second sentence contains the main idea: There are many reasons why students become distance learners. (Par. 6, lines 2–3)

bachelor's
bachelor's; first degree at a college or university (Par. 7)

people learn
Claim: The future for alternative education looks very strong. (Par. 8, line 1)

MAIN IDEA CHECK (page 67)

Paragraphs 1–4
A 4 **B** 2 **C** 1 **D** 3
Paragraphs 5–8
E 6 **F** 8 **G** 7 **H** 5

A CLOSER LOOK (page 68)

1 True

2 Paragraph 3 describes High Tech High, a school that Bill Gates might like for these reasons:
(1) Students learn from computers – there are no textbooks. (Par. 3, lines 11–12)
(2) As in Montessori classrooms, students learn actively by planning and building their own projects. Instead of taking tests, they are evaluated on their projects. (Par. 3, lines 12–14)
(3) In addition to classwork, all students have to work in a high-tech business. (Par. 3, lines 14–15)

3 a (Par. 2, lines 6–10); c (Par. 2, lines 5–6)

4 Answers will vary.
Main idea: Parents choose homeschooling for many different reasons. (Par. 4, line 3)
Supporting detail: Some disagree with standardized tests and do not like a traditional curriculum. (Par. 4, lines 4–5)
Supporting detail: Others choose to homeschool because they want to emphasize religious and moral instruction. (Par. 4, lines 5–6)
Supporting detail: Many parents also see homeschooling as an opportunity to spend more time with their children. (Par. 4, lines 6–8)

5 False (Par. 5, lines 3–4)

6 Answers will vary.
Main idea: A growing number of families are choosing homeschooling. (Par. 5, lines 1–2)
Supporting detail: It is estimated that Canada has about 80,000 homeschool families. (Par. 5, lines 2–3)
Supporting detail: In Great Britain . . . from about 12,000 in 1999 to over 50,000 in 2005. (Par. 5, lines 3–4)
Supporting detail: The United States . . . over 1 million children homeschooled each year. (Par. 5, lines 4–6)

7 b (Par. 6, lines 6–7)

8 False (Par. 7, lines 2–3)

9 (1) People are dissatisfied with traditional education. (Par. 8, lines 1–5)
(2) As technology continues to change, people will develop new forms of schooling. (Par. 8, lines 5–7)

VOCABULARY STUDY: SYNONYMS (page 69)

1 criticize(ing) **2** concerned **3** approaches **4** emotional **5** encourage(d) **6** particularly **7** projects
8 growing **9** location **10** likely

VOCABULARY STUDY: WORDS IN CONTEXT (page 69)

1 passive **2** concentrate **3** dissatisfied **4** physical **5** obsolete **6** High-tech **7** shortage **8** designed
9 actively **10** Alternative

READING 4 SKILLS FOR THE TWENTY-FIRST CENTURY

GETTING A FIRST IDEA ABOUT THE ARTICLE (page 71)

SECTION	TOPIC
II	A description of skills people need today
IV	An evaluation of how different countries are teaching twenty-first-century skills
V	An explanation of why twenty-first-century skills are essential
III	An explanation about how people use skills while they are working
I	Background information about how literacy and skills have changed through history

WHILE YOU READ (pages 72–75)

needed in the past
Topic: (Twenty-first-century job skills) (Par. 1, line 13)
Claim: are very different from the skills people needed in the past. (Par. 1, lines 13–14)

three things
(1) First, they can find information from different sources such as texts, videos, audio files, and databases (Par. 2, lines 5–6)
(2) Next, . . . evaluate these sources to make sure the information is current and accurate (Par. 2, lines 6–8)
(3) Finally, . . . use a range of technology tools and software programs to present their research (Par. 2, lines 9–11)

many skills
Main idea: (Good communication includes many skills.) (Par. 3, lines 1–2)
Supporting details:
(1) People must . . . talk or write about their ideas so that others can clearly understand them (Par. 3, lines 2–3)
(2) In addition, . . . working well in a group (Par. 3, lines 3–4)
(3) Lastly, . . . knowing how to work with people from different cultures (Par. 3, lines 7–8)

inventive
creative (Par. 4, line 2)

these critical thinking skills
to think and ask questions about what they learn (Par. 4, lines 4–5)

launch
Launch is a noun in this sentence. Students should underline its. (Par. 5, line 14)

investors

Par. 6, lines 8–9, provide context clues; people who lend money to help a business start or grow

On the other hand

Only 6 percent of Internet users live in Africa or the Middle East (Par. 7, lines 5–6); almost 20 percent live in the United States and Canada, and over 90 percent of the world's Internet users are in industrialized countries. (Par. 7, lines 7–10)

second language

Main idea: Countries where English . . . successful in teaching a second language. (Par. 9, lines 1–2)
Supporting details:
(1) Compared to China, . . . a much smaller number of American children learn a second language (Par. 9, lines 2–3)
(2) Moreover, . . . most of these students do not speak a second language as well as students from other countries speak English (Par. 9, lines 5–7)
(3) Finally, . . . the number of Americans studying in other countries . . . is still low (Par. 9, lines 8–9)

MAIN IDEA CHECK (page 75)

Paragraphs 1–4
A 3 **B** 1 **C** 4 **D** 2

Paragraphs 5–6
E 6 **F** 5

Paragraphs 7–11
G 9 **H** 7 **I** 10 **J** 11 **K** 8

A CLOSER LOOK (page 76)

1 b (Par. 1, lines 6–9)
2 False (Par. 2, lines 1–4)
3 c (Par. 3, lines 7–10)
4 a, b, e (Pars. 5–6)
5 Answers will vary.
   Main idea: Students all over the world learn English. (Par. 8, lines 2–3)
   Supporting detail: . . . over a billion people now speak English as either a first or a second language. (Par. 8, lines 3–5)
   Supporting detail: In European countries, children . . . learn English in primary school, and in China . . . at the age of eight. (Par. 8, lines 5–7)
   Supporting detail: In addition, . . . thousands of students travel to English-speaking countries to improve their English. (Par. 8, lines 7–9)
6 c (Par. 10, lines 1–6)
7 d (Par. 10, lines 9–11)
8 True (Par. 11, lines 6–8)

VOCABULARY STUDY: SYNONYMS (page 77)

1 spread **2** databases **3** current **4** range **5** incorporate **6** launch **7** encounter(ed) **8** (to) lend
9 regions **10** fluent

VOCABULARY STUDY: WORD FAMILIES (pages 77–78)

1 analyzed **2** memories **3** collaboration **4** curiosity **5** memorized **6** requirement **7** collaborated
8 required **9** analysis **10** curious

VOCABULARY REVIEW: SAME OR DIFFERENT (page 78)

1 D **2** D **3** S **4** S **5** S **6** S

MAKING CONNECTIONS

EXERCISE 1 (pages 80–81)

1 They parents
    they parents

2 This The fastest growing type of alternative education is distance learning.
    it distance learning

3 They students
    this to collaborate
    it final project

4 it Google Web site

5 it Primary education
    This Primary education is compulsory in most countries, and it is usually free.

EXERCISE 2 (pages 81–82)

1 B, A, C
2 C, A, B
3 B, A, C
4 C, A, B
5 B, C, A

UNIT 3 The World of Business

SKILLS AND STRATEGIES 5 THE VOCABULARY OF NUMBERS

SKILL PRACTICE 1 (page 85)

Answers will vary.
1 increased / rose / grew; increase
2 fell / declined / dropped / went down
3 rapidly / significantly / sharply / dramatically
4 grew / increased / rose
5 grew / increased / rose

SKILL PRACTICE 2 (page 86)

Answers will vary.
1 The cost of eggs increased from 18 cents per dozen to 71 cents per dozen.
2 The cost fell sharply from 71 cents per dozen to 39 cents.
3 The cost rose dramatically from 39 cents per dozen to 91 cents.
4 The cost increased from 91 cents to 2 dollars and 17 cents.
5 I think the cost will continue to rise steadily in the future.

SKILL PRACTICE 3 (page 86)

Answers will vary, but students should include a variety of vocabulary from page 84.

READING 1 SUPPLY AND DEMAND IN THE GLOBAL ECONOMY

GETTING A FIRST IDEA ABOUT THE ARTICLE (page 87)

1 coffee
2 100 cups per month
3 40 cups per month
4 People buy more coffee when the price is low.

WHILE YOU READ (pages 88–89)

there is a growth in demand
   rose (Par. 1, line 8); increase (Par. 1, line 10); increased (Par. 2, line 2)

The law of demand
   as prices rise, demand falls (Par. 3, lines 9–10)

supply
   product to sell (Par. 4, line 2)

doubled
   decreased by approximately 33 percent (Par. 5, line 6); corn skyrocketed to its highest price in ten years (Par. 5, lines 8–9); the price of corn doubled in March 2007 (Par. 5, line 14)

MAIN IDEA CHECK (page 90)
A 6 **B** 2 **C** 4 **D** 1 **E** 5 **F** 3

A CLOSER LOOK (pages 90–91)

1 c (Par. 1, lines 2–4)
2 c (Par. 3, lines 8–9; 10–12)
3 False (Par. 4, lines 8–10)
4

```
[ B ] → [ D ] → [ E ] → [ A ] → [ C ]
```

5 d (Par. 5, lines 5–9)
6 because of the increasing need for alternative fuels, such as ethanol (Par. 5, lines 3–5)

VOCABULARY STUDY: SYNONYMS (page 91)

1 plants **2** produce(d) **3** crop **4** effect **5** approximately **6** skyrocket(ed) **7** import(s) **8** survive(s)
9 ingredient **10** protest(ing)

VOCABULARY STUDY: WORDS IN CONTEXT (pages 91–92)

1 event **2** surplus **3** energy **4** affects **5** flapping **6** sayings **7** note **8** previously
9 Consumption **10** fuel

READING 2 THE WORKFORCE OF THE TWENTY-FIRST CENTURY

GETTING A FIRST IDEA ABOUT THE ARTICLE (page 93)
Answers will vary.

SECTION	HEADING	QUESTION
I	Supply and Demand for Skilled Workers	What is a skilled worker?
		A person who has technology skills
II	Outsourcing: A Practice That Saves Money	What is outsourcing?
		When companies move parts of their business to other countries
III	A Mobile, Global Workforce	What is a mobile workforce?
		A workforce that is willing to move to another place for work

WHILE YOU READ (pages 94–96)
an increasing number
an increasing number (Par. 2, line 5)
go down (Par. 2, line 9)
losing (Par. 3, line 3)
loss (Par. 3, line 4)
lose (Par. 3, line 6)
gain (Par. 3, line 7)
fell (Par. 3, line 8)

this
today's workers are willing to move away from home in order to get a good job (Par. 4, lines 2–3)

find work
Main idea: (some governments are trying to help workers to move to their countries) (Par. 5, lines 3–4)
Supporting details:
(1) Countries . . . for skilled people to move to these countries. (Par. 5, lines 5–7)
(2) They are also trying to encourage . . . stay in these countries after they graduate. (Par. 5, lines 7–9)

windows and seats
At that time (Par. 7, line 3); Today (Par. 7, line 4); now (Par. 7, line 9)

MAIN IDEA CHECK (page 96)

Paragraphs 1–3
A 2   **B** 3   **C** 1

Paragraphs 4–7
D 7   **E** 4   **F** 5   **G** 6

A CLOSER LOOK (pages 96–97)

1 b (Par. 1, lines 4–5)

2 A – For the company that outsources (Par. 2, lines 9–10)
A – For workers in developing countries (Par. 3, line 1)
D – For workers in developed countries (Par. 3, lines 3–5)

3 True (Par. 3, lines 7–9)

4 c (Par. 4)

5 a (Par. 5, lines 2–3); c (Par. 6, lines 1–4)

6 a, b, c, d (Par. 6)

7 False (Par. 7, lines 2–6)

VOCABULARY STUDY: SYNONYMS (page 97)

1 salaries   **2** housing   **3** developing   **4** willing   **5** practice   **6** blame   **7** gain   **8** specialists
9 workforce   **10** hire

VOCABULARY STUDY: WORD FAMILIES (page 98)

1 manufactures   **2** flexible   **3** comfortable   **4** attractive   **5** flexibility   **6** attract   **7** Manufacturing
8 prevention   **9** Comfort   **10** prevents

VOCABULARY REVIEW: SAME OR DIFFERENT (page 99)

1 D   **2** S   **3** D   **4** D   **5** S   **6** D

SKILLS AND STRATEGIES 6   INFORMATION IN GRAPHS AND CHARTS

SKILL PRACTICE 1 (page 102)

1 coal   **2** oil   **3** b

SKILL PRACTICE 2 (page 103)

1 4   **2** 19 million   **3** 844 million   **4** 656 million   **5** 500 million   **6** 675 million   **7** 1.344 billion

SKILL PRACTICE 3 (pages 104–105)

1 A "green" workplace is a healthy working environment that does not use much energy and water and does not produce much waste and pollution.

2 It is an independent organization that certifies "green" businesses.

3 791

4 2006–2007

5 by adding all the numbers from each year

6 It is healthier for people to work in a green workplace.

READING 3   COMMUNICATION TECHNOLOGY AND GLOBAL BUSINESS

GETTING A FIRST IDEA ABOUT THE ARTICLE (page 106)

QUESTION	FIGURE 3.3	FIGURE 3.4
1. What is the title?	Internet Use: Percent of the Population in 2007	Gross National Income (GNI) per Person in U.S. dollars
2. What information is in the vertical axis?	Percentage of the population	U.S. dollars
3. What information is in the horizontal axis?	Countries	Same countries
4. Which country had the highest percentage of their population use the Internet in 2007? What was the percentage?	Sweden; about 75%	
5. Which country had the lowest percentage of their population use the Internet in 2007? What was the percentage?	India; about 3%	
6. In which country does the average person have the highest GNI? What is the amount?		United States; $45,000 U.S. dollars
7. In which country does the average person have the lowest GNI? What is the amount?		Vietnam; about $1,000 U.S. dollars

WHILE YOU READ (pages 107–109)

instant messaging, blogs, and social networking sites
   let people work together more efficiently (Par. 2, lines 5–6); allow them to collect and share different kinds of information in text, pictures, audio, and video (Par. 2, lines 6–7)

distribute tasks
   One good example is the motorcycle manufacturing industry in China. (Par. 4, lines 7–8)

make it possible
   by using blogs and social networking sites, such as Facebook, Orkut, or Cyworld (Par. 5, lines 7–9)

be connected
   Experts are connected by the Internet. (Par. 6)

MAIN IDEA CHECK (page 110)

Paragraphs 1–4
A 3   **B** 4   **C** 1   **D** 2
Paragraphs 5–7
E 6   **F** 7   **G** 5

A CLOSER LOOK (pages 110–111)

1 (1) instant messaging; (2) blogs; (3) social networking sites (Par. 2, lines 4–5)
2 c
3 c
4 False (Par. 4, lines 13–15)
5 changes as a result of new ideas (Par. 6, lines 1–3)
6 b, c, and e (Par. 6, lines 4–9)
7 b (Par. 7, lines 2–4)
8 b

VOCABULARY STUDY: SYNONYMS (page 111)

1 key **2** (to) interact **3** (to) share **4** team **5** members **6** constant **7** effective **8** reward
9 suggestions **10** promote

VOCABULARY STUDY: WORDS IN CONTEXT (page 112)

1 distributed **2** mining **3** expert **4** prosperity **5** role **6** tools **7** tasks **8** innovation
9 participation **10** Fortunately

READING 4   BUSINESS AND SUSTAINABILITY

GETTING A FIRST IDEA ABOUT THE ARTICLE (page 113)
Answers will vary.

SECTION	PARAGRAPH	QUESTION
I	1	How are people harming the world?
II	2	What are sustainable products?
	3	How many people use solar energy?
	5	Which familiar products are sustainable?
III	7	What other changes are businesses making?
	9	What are the two reasons why businesses are changing?
	10	Is sustainability profitable?

WHILE YOU READ (pages 114–117)
concerns
  (1) using up natural resources (Par. 1, lines 2–3)
  (2) polluting the water and air (Par. 1, lines 4–5)
  (3) climate change (Par. 1, line 6)

(See Figure 3.5.)
  Answers will vary.
  Fossil fuel emissions are increasing steadily.

sustainable use of resources
  (1) In . . . using energy from the sun to heat our homes . . . (Par. 3, lines 1–3)
  (2) The use of *gray water* is another example of a sustainable process. (Par. 3, lines 5–6)

several ways
  Main idea: (Businesses are responding to these environmental concerns in several ways.)
  (Par. 4, lines 1–2)
  Supporting examples:
  (1) the hybrid car (Par. 4, line 5)
  (2) wind and solar power (Par. 4, line 13)

organic
  grown without chemicals (Par. 6, line 3)

protect the environment
  Topic: (Recycling) (Par. 8, line 1)
  Claim: is another way that businesses can help protect the environment (Par. 8, lines 1–2)

two main reasons
  (1) First, this can save money. (Par. 9, line 3)
  (2) The second reason . . . is that it can improve a company's image. (Par. 9, lines 6–7)

MAIN IDEA CHECK (pages 117–118)

Paragraphs 1–6
A 2 **B** 5 **C** 1 **D** 4 **E** 3 **F** 6
Paragraphs 7–10
G 7 **H** 10 **I** 8 **J** 9

A CLOSER LOOK (pages 118–119)

1 c (Par. 1, lines 5–9)
2 (1) it pollutes the air (Par. 2, line 7); (2) it uses oil, a nonrenewable resource (Par. 2, lines 8–9); (3) cars emit CO_2 into the air, contributing to global warming (Par. 2, lines 9–11)
3 D → C → B → A
4 b (Figure 3.5)
5 the dirty water after washing dishes, laundry, or taking showers, etc. (Par. 3, lines 5–7)
6 False (Par. 4, lines 8–10) **7** d **8** a (Par. 5, lines 13–15); c (Par. 5, lines 15–16)
9 b and c (Pars. 7 and 9) **10** False (Par. 10, lines 9–13)

VOCABULARY STUDY: SYNONYMS (page 119)

1 us(ing) up **2** resources **3** climate **4** droughts **5** eventually **6** (will) run out **7** bamboo **8** organic
9 snack **10** image

VOCABULARY STUDY: WORD FAMILIES (page 120)

1 damage (n) **2** donate **3** emission **4** pollution **5** damage (v) **6** recycle **7** donations **8** Recycling
9 emit **10** pollute

VOCABULARY REVIEW: SAME OR DIFFERENT (page 121)

1 S **2** D **3** S **4** D **5** S **6** D

MAKING CONNECTIONS

EXERCISE 1 (pages 122–123)

2 Rising oil prices can cause changes in the price of other energy sources. Corn is an alternative source of energy. So as oil prices rose, some businesses started to produce ethanol, a fuel made from corn. As a result of growing demand, corn prices increased dramatically.

3 A decline in the economy can be good for education. When the economy is good, there are lots of jobs that pay well. As a result, students leave school to find jobs. When the economy declines, there are fewer jobs, so students stay in school.

4 Some investors have a simple plan for success. One of these investors is (Warren Buffet). (He) buys (companies) for a good price, and then (he) keeps (them) for a long time. This strategy has been a great success, and as a result, today Buffet is a very rich man.

5 In today's economy, jobs can often move around the world. (Global businesses) want to keep (their) labor costs low. So, if the cost of labor in one country is too high, (they) may move (their) factories to another country where labor is cheaper. This practice is called *outsourcing* and can result in unemployment in the countries with higher labor costs.

EXERCISE 2 (pages 123–124)

1 A, C, B
2 B, C, A
3 C, B, A
4 B, A, C
5 B, A, C

UNIT 4 Population Change and Its Impact

SKILLS AND STRATEGIES 7 INCREASING READING SPEED

SKILL PRACTICE 1 (page 127)

1 People leave to find greater security.
2 Others leave to find more political and religious freedom.

SKILL PRACTICE 2 (page 128)

Answers will vary.

   When people arrive / in a new country, / they are called immigrants. / One important reason / immigrants come to a new country / is economics. / Immigrants usually choose a country / that has better opportunities than their homeland: more land, / more jobs, / or better pay. / They may also hope to find / better working and living conditions, / better health care for their families, / and a better education for their children. / Some people / leave their home country / because of dangers there, / and they believe / they will be safer / in the new country. / Finally, / immigrants may choose a new country / where they will be freer / to express their ideas / or to practice their religion.

SKILL PRACTICE 3 (page 128)

1 The government and people in a country do not always welcome immigrants.
2 They may limit the number of people who can come, or they may require a certain amount of money or education.
3 They may think immigrants are a danger to their culture, language, and financial security.

READING 1 POPULATION TRENDS

GETTING A FIRST IDEA ABOUT THE ARTICLE (page 129)

Answers will vary.
1 It shows population growth in developing and developed countries.
2 It suggests that population growth will be highest in developing countries.
3 Answers will vary.

BIG FAMILY	SMALL FAMILY
5 children	2 children
poor clothes	nice clothes
unhappy	happy
fighting	school bag
bare tree	tractor

4 Smaller families are happier, are better educated, and have more money than larger families.

WHILE YOU READ (pages 130–132)

Demography is the study of population.

   Answers will vary.

   Demography is the study of population. / It can tell us / the percentage of a country's population / in a specific age range, / for example, / whether there are more people over / or under 65. / Demography is also the study of population trends. / These trends / include increases or decreases /

in a country's population. / This information is important / because changes in population / can have an enormous impact / on a country's future. / One important demographic trend / is that the world's population / has been growing rapidly / since the nineteenth century. / However, / this change is not the same / in all parts of the world. / The population of the developing world / is growing much faster / than the population of the developed world. (Par. 1)

Two factors

life expectancy (Par. 2, line 2); fertility rate (Par. 3, line 1)

fertility rate

The fertility rate is the average number of children per woman. (Par. 3, lines 1–2)

(See Figure 4.2.)

Middle East / North Africa had the largest decrease of 3.9 children per woman.

lots of resources

Main idea: (As a result, some of these countries made great efforts to control their population growth by encouraging people to have smaller families.) (Par. 4, lines 3–5)

a major concern is the decline in population

(1) In Japan and in most of Europe, fertility rates are now too low to replace the current population. (Par. 6, lines 2–3)

(2) This falling fertility rate is a problem because younger workers have to support the older, retired population. Soon there will not be enough workers, and there will be too many retired people. (Par. 6, lines 6–9)

maternity leave

the time a woman takes off from work when she has a baby (Par. 7)

MAIN IDEA CHECK (page 133)

Paragraphs 1–4

A 2   **B** 1   **C** 4   **D** 3

Paragraphs 5–7

E 7   **F** 5   **G** 6

A CLOSER LOOK (pages 133–134)

1 b

2 The two most important factors are life expectancy (Par. 2, line 2) and fertility rate (Par. 3, line 1).

3 3.6 Asia
   1.3 Europe
   3.4 Latin America / Caribbean
   3.9 Middle East / North Africa
   1.5 North America
   1.3 Sub-Saharan Africa

4 b (Par. 3, lines 6–8)

5 b (Par. 4, lines 9–11)

6 False (Par. 6, lines 4–6)

7 b (Par. 6, lines 6–9)

8 a (Par. 7, lines 2–5); c (Par. 7, lines 7–10); e (Par. 7, lines 5–7)

VOCABULARY STUDY: SYNONYMS (page 134)

1 population   **2** trends   **3** figures   **4** support   **5** efforts   **6** financial   **7** penalties   **8** explosion
9 (to) replace   **10** retired

VOCABULARY STUDY: WORDS IN CONTEXT (page 135)

1 single   **2** agriculture   **3** Demography   **4** child care   **5** Life expectancy   **6** According to
7 maternity leave   **8** hygiene   **9** fertility rate   **10** existing

READING 2 GLOBAL MIGRATION

GETTING A FIRST IDEA ABOUT THE ARTICLE (page 136)

Answers will vary.

PARAGRAPH	QUESTION
3	Which countries do immigrants move to?
4	How many immigrants move to countries that are only a little more prosperous than their homeland?
5	Are some immigrants wealthy and educated?
6	What is the impact of migration?

WHILE YOU READ (pages 137–138)

In today's global economy
  Answers will vary.

country of origin
  the country where you are born and grow up (Par. 1)

host country
  the country immigrants move to (Par. 2)

prosperous
  prosperous is an adjective; wealthy; successful (Par. 4)

This impact can be positive
  Main idea: This impact can be positive for both the host country and the immigrants' homeland.
  (Par. 6, lines 2–3)
  Supporting details:
  (1) Many countries have a shortage of workers. In these countries . . . that do not require a
       specific skill. (Par. 6, lines 3–5)
  (2) They can also allow skilled workers in the host country to be more productive. (Par. 6, lines 5–6)
  (3) Migration can also help the immigrants' homeland . . . send part of their income back to their
       families in their home country. (Par. 6, lines 9–11)

are not always positive
  Main idea: The economic and social effects are not always positive, however. (Par. 7, lines 1–2)
  Supporting details:
  (1) For the . . . services for immigrants, such as health care and education, are expensive.
       (Par. 7, lines 2–3)
  (2) Some . . . fear that immigrants will take their jobs away. (Par. 7, lines 3–5)
  (3) In addition, if the cultures . . . are very different . . . misunderstandings between the two groups.
       (Par. 7, lines 5–7)
  (4) However, . . . the immigrants' homelands . . . lose their most productive workers. (Par. 7, lines 7–9)
  (5) Migration . . . can divide families . . . (Par. 7, line 9)
  (6) . . . leave towns and villages almost empty. (Par. 7, lines 9–10)
  (7) Finally, . . . immigrants . . . do not invest in their homelands. (Par. 7, lines 10–12)

MAIN IDEA CHECK (page 139)

Paragraphs 1–4
A 4 **B** 1 **C** 2 **D** 3
Paragraphs 5–7
E 7 **F** 5 **G** 6

A CLOSER LOOK (pages 139–140)

1 <u>3</u> Asia
  <u>1</u> Europe
  <u>2</u> North America
2 hope for a better life (Par. 2, lines 4–5)
3 b (Par. 4, lines 3–4)
4 True (Par. 4, lines 6–7)
5 b (Par. 5, lines 1–5)
6

POSITIVE EFFECTS	NEGATIVE EFFECTS
Immigrants fill shortage of workers. (Par. 6, lines 3–5)	Health care and education for immigrants are expensive. (Par. 7, lines 2–3)
Immigrants help skilled workers be more productive. (Par. 6, lines 5–6)	Some fear immigrants will take away jobs. (Par. 7, lines 3–5)
Immigrants help their homeland by sending money back. (Par. 6, lines 9–11)	There may be misunderstandings due to different cultures. (Par. 7, lines 5–7)
	Immigrants' homelands lose workers. (Par. 7, lines 8–9)
	Families may be divided. (Par. 7, line 9)
	Towns and villages may be empty. (Par. 7, lines 9–10)
	Immigrants may not invest in their homelands. (Par. 7, lines 10–12)

VOCABULARY STUDY: SYNONYMS (page 140)

1 borders **2** forces **3** immigrants **4** typical **5** prosperous **6** homeland **7** income **8** widespread **9** allow **10** invest

VOCABULARY STUDY: WORD FAMILIES (pages 140–141)

1 wealthy **2** original **3** migration **4** intention **5** wealth **6** permit **7** origin **8** intend **9** migrate **10** permission

VOCABULARY REVIEW: SAME OR DIFFERENT (pages 141–142)

1 S **2** D **3** S **4** D **5** D **6** S

SKILLS AND STRATEGIES 8 SCANNING FOR SPECIFIC INFORMATION

SKILL PRACTICE 1 (page 144)

1 Beijing **2** London **3** Mumbai (formerly Bombay) **4** over 25 million people

SKILL PRACTICE 2 (page 145)

1 <u>Thomas Malthus</u>; English economist who was interested in demography
2 <u>overpopulation</u>; 1798
3 <u>*Malthusians*</u>; people who agree with Malthus's theory that there would not be enough food for everyone unless population growth was slowed
4 <u>reduce</u>; war, disease, or smaller families

SKILL PRACTICE 3 (page 146)

1 70% **2** 443 hours **3** two-thirds **4** $63 billion

READING 3 THE GROWTH OF CITIES

GETTING A FIRST IDEA ABOUT THE ARTICLE (page 147)
A 3 **B** 5 **C** 1 **D** 4 **E** 2 **F** 6

WHILE YOU READ (pages 148–149)
In 1800
50% (Par. 1, line 3)

different reasons
(1) The first cities grew up around marketplaces . . . large rivers or around harbors. (Par. 2, lines 1–4)
(2) As religions built . . . around important religious buildings. (Par. 2, lines 5–6)
(3) Later, . . . became the centers for government. (Par. 2, lines 6–7)
(4) They also provided security . . . surrounded by walls. (Par. 2, lines 7–8)
(5) Finally, . . . attracted . . . people with ideas about art and science . . . became centers for culture. (Par. 2, lines 9–11)

differently
North American cities (Par. 4, line 1) and European cities (Par. 4, line 5)

Today
cities in developing countries (Par. 5, line 1) and cities in Europe (Par. 5, line 2)

growing urban population
Main idea: Yet cities share one thing: people move to cities looking for opportunities.
(Par. 6, lines 4–5)

MAIN IDEA CHECK (page 149)
A 5 **B** 4 **C** 6 **D** 3 **E** 2 **F** 1

A CLOSER LOOK (pages 150–151)
1 a 3% (Par. 1, line 1)
  b 4.9 billion (Par. 1, line 7)
  c Ernest Burgess (Par. 4, line 2)
  d millions (Par. 5, line 10)

2 False (Par. 1, lines 5–7)

3 Main idea: There are several reasons why cities developed. (Students should include four of the five below.)
Supporting detail: grew up around marketplaces (Par. 2, line 2)
Supporting detail: were built around important religious buildings (Par. 2, line 6)
Supporting detail: became the centers for government (Par. 2, line 7)
Supporting detail: provided security in a dangerous world (Par. 2, lines 7–8)
Supporting detail: attracted people with ideas about art and science (Par. 2, lines 10–11)

4 b (Par. 5, lines 2–3); e (Par. 4, lines 7–9)

5

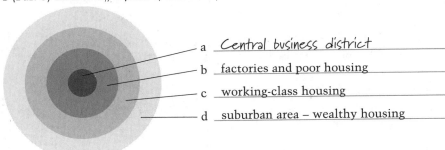

a Central business district
b factories and poor housing
c working-class housing
d suburban area – wealthy housing

6 True (Par. 4, lines 7–9)

7 b (Par. 5, lines 5–9)

8 water (Par. 5, line 9) and electricity (Par. 5, line 10)

VOCABULARY STUDY: SYNONYMS (page 151)

1 urban   **2** predict(s)   **3** trade(d)   **4** sector   **5** suburbs   **6** pattern   **7** sociologist   **8** series
9 residents   **10** vibrant

VOCABULARY STUDY: WORDS IN CONTEXT (pages 151–152)

1 face   **2** squatter settlements   **3** by hand   **4** harbor   **5** rural   **6** astounding   **7** surrounded   **8** evolved
9 working class   **10** model

READING 4   CHALLENGES FACING THE WORLD'S CITIES

GETTING A FIRST IDEA ABOUT THE ARTICLE (page 153)

SECTION	TOPIC
III	Traffic problems in major cities
III	Breathing problems for residents of cities with bad air pollution
II	People who are too poor to find housing and who have to live on the streets
IV	New smaller communities that use alternative energy
IV	Planning for better urban living in the next century
II	Reasons that the crime rate is so high in some cities
I	The largest cities in the past and in the future
I	A definition of megacities

WHILE YOU READ (pages154–157)

cities have offered hope and opportunity
cities with a population of more than 10 million people (Par. 1, line 5)

This urbanization
the spread and growth of cities (Par. 1)

reasons
(1) Some are mentally ill; . . . (Par. 2, line 10)
(2) . . . others are drug or alcohol addicts. (Par. 2, line 10)
(3) Mostly, . . . homeless are the very poor who cannot afford to buy or rent a place to live
(Par. 2, lines 11–13)

rapid urbanization
Main idea: (Historically, crime is most likely to rise during periods of rapid urbanization.)
(Par. 5, lines 1–2)
Supporting details:
(1) Often they cannot find jobs . . . live in difficult conditions. (Par. 5, lines 6–7)
(2) During periods of rapid urbanization . . . near each other. (Par. 5, lines 10–11)

"smart growth"
A community in South London, England (Par. 9, line 1); China (Par. 9, line 12)

hybrid cars
• smaller communities with parks and gardens
• use of alternative energies
• services and employment near where people live so they can walk to work

- green areas where people can plant trees, flowers, and vegetables
- efficient public transportation (Par. 8, lines 9–14)

where they often face difficult living conditions

Main idea: (People all around the world are making changes in their cities.) (Par. 10, lines 7–8)

MAIN IDEA CHECK (page 157)

Paragraphs 1–5

A 4 **B** 3 **C** 5 **D** 2 **E** 1

Paragraphs 6–10

F 9 **G** 10 **H** 6 **I** 8 **J** 7

A CLOSER LOOK (page 158)

1 a 35 (Par. 1, line 6)
  b Tokyo, Japan (Table 4.1)
  c over 1 million (Par. 3, line 9)
  d five and a half million (Par. 6, lines 5–6)
  e Cubatão (Par. 7, line 4)

2 False (Table 4.1)

3 a

4 c (Par. 3, lines 4–6)

5 True (Par. 5, lines 1–2)

6 c

7 False (Par. 7, lines 4–6)

8 a, c, d, e (Pars. 8–9)

VOCABULARY STUDY: SYNONYMS (page 159)

1 (have) offer(ed) **2** poverty **3** homeless **4** (to) beg **5** unique **6** cemetery **7** tombs **8** victims
9 cancer **10** principles

VOCABULARY STUDY: WORD FAMILIES (pages 159–160)

1 respiration **2** buried **3** inequality **4** ill **5** burial **6** respiratory **7** similarities **8** unequal
9 illnesses **10** similar

VOCABULARY REVIEW: SAME OR DIFFERENT (page 160)

1 S **2** D **3** S **4** D **5** S **6** S

MAKING CONNECTIONS

EXERCISE 1 (pages 162–163)

1   The definition of a city is (an urban settlement) that has (its) own government. (This government) provides important (services) to (its) residents. (They) include schools, water, electricity, and roads. Although all cities provide (these services) to some people, many cities cannot provide (them) to everyone.

2   (All countries) have experienced some changes in (their) population growth. This growth has occurred at different times in different parts of the world. Europe and North America had an explosion in population growth in the early nineteenth century. In contrast, many African and Latin American countries began to grow rapidly in the twentieth century.

3   Better <u>hygiene</u> and <u>health care</u> have increased <u>life expectancy</u> in many <u>countries</u>. A simple change, the introduction of soap in the nineteeth century, made a <u>big difference</u> in <u>life expectancy</u>. Medicines that prevent disease have made an even <u>bigger difference</u>. However, there are still some <u>countries</u> today where <u>life expectancy</u> is <u>low</u> because of the <u>low</u> standard of <u>hygiene</u> and <u>health care</u>.

4   How do we know the <u>population</u> of different <u>countries</u>? (Some <u>countries</u>), like Canada and England, count (their) <u>inhabitants</u> every ten <u>years</u>. In contrast, France <u>counts</u> every seven <u>years</u>, and (Japan and Australia) <u>count</u> (their) <u>inhabitants</u> every five <u>years</u>. This information provides an estimate of the worldwide <u>population</u>.

5   People <u>immigrate</u> for <u>different</u> reasons. (Most people) leave (their) <u>homelands</u> for economic <u>reasons</u>. Another <u>reason</u> is that (parents) want a better education for (their) children. Although (their) <u>reasons</u> for <u>leaving</u> (their) <u>homelands</u> are often <u>different</u>, (all <u>immigrants</u>) hope to find a better life.

EXERCISE 2 (pages 163-164)
1 C, A, B
2 A, C, B
3 C, A, B
4 C, B, A
5 C, B, A

UNIT 5 Design in Everyday Life

SKILLS AND STRATEGIES 9 VOCABULARY STUDY

SKILL PRACTICE 1 (page 167)
Answers will vary. The vocabulary cards should look like the examples from page 167.

SKILL PRACTICE 2 (page 168)
Answers will vary. The vocabulary cards should look like the examples from page 167.

SKILL PRACTICE 3 (page 168)
Answers will vary. The vocabulary cards should look like the examples from page 167.

READING 1 THE DESIGN OF EVERYDAY OBJECTS

GETTING A FIRST IDEA ABOUT THE ARTICLE (page 169)
Answers will vary.
1 I think you put the lemon on the top of the lemon squeezer. Then you squeeze it.
2 It is well designed because it looks very simple to use.
3 Yes, I would buy it. It looks simple and attractive.
4 I think the chair looks poorly designed. It looks very uncomfortable.
5 No, I would not buy it. It looks like art, not a chair.

WHILE YOU READ (pages 170–172)
fine
    beautiful and expensive; good quality (Par. 2)

stores
    stores is a verb; to keep things in order to use them in the future (Par. 3)

One design expert
    Main idea: (One design expert . . . usability.) (Par. 5, lines 1–2)
    Supporting details:
    (1) According to . . . products should provide visual signs. (Par. 5, lines 3–4)
    (2) A product should also tell the users if they have used it correctly. (Par. 5, lines 6–7)
    (3) Finally, . . . should prevent users from doing something wrong. (Par. 5, lines 8–9)

Functionality and usability
    Main idea: (Functionality and usability are central design principles, but there is one more very important consideration – the *emotional response* to the product.) (Par. 7, lines 1–3)

small, fast sports car
    Answers will vary.
    A big car says that a person is rich and likes to be safe. A small sports car says that a person is rich, young, and likes to take risks. (Par. 8)

the person who wears it
    Answers will vary. (Par. 9)

MAIN IDEA CHECK (page 173)

Paragraphs 1–5
A 2   **B** 4   **C** 3   **D** 1   **E** 5
Paragraphs 6–9
F 7   **G** 9   **H** 6   **I** 8

A CLOSER LOOK (pages 173–174)

1 d (Par. 2, lines 8–9)
2 False (Par. 3)
3 Answers will vary. Some high-tech cell phones and clocks are too hard to use.
4 b (Par. 5, lines 3–4); d (Par. 4, lines 1–3); e (Par. 5, lines 6–7)
5 a (Par. 6, lines 4–7)
6 Answers will vary. Watch #2 is the most usable because it looks basic and easy to use. Watch #3 is the least usable. It is difficult to tell the time on this watch.
7 False

VOCABULARY STUDY: SYNONYMS (page 174)

1 carve(d)   **2** complex   **3** basic   **4** visual   **5** horizontal   **6** vertical   **7** occur   **8** persuade
9 pleasure   **10** leather

VOCABULARY STUDY: WORDS IN CONTEXT (pages 174–175)

1 changed his mind   **2** oven   **3** decorated   **4** mass-produced   **5** preference   **6** confusing   **7** owner
8 indicate   **9** craftsmen   **10** identity

READING 2   ERGONOMICS

GETTING A FIRST IDEA ABOUT THE ARTICLE (page 176)

	FIGURE 5.1	PHOTO
Feet flat on the floor	✓	
Back straight	✓	
Arms supported	✓	
Back supported	✓	
Computer screen at eye level	✓	

Answers will vary.
I think it's best to have your back straight and feet flat on the floor.

WHILE YOU READ (pages 177–179)
thumbs
   the short finger of each hand

two main principles
   (1) The first principle is efficiency. (Par. 2, lines 1–2)
   (2) The second principle is human comfort. (Par. 2, line 4)

workstation
   desk, chair, and computer (Par. 3, line 2)

monitor; keyboard; forearms; back; wrists

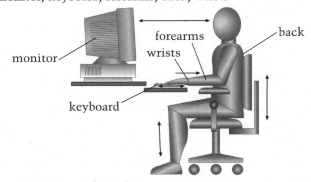

worse

Main idea: (Doctors . . . but they say laptop computers are making the problems even worse.)
(Par. 5, lines 1–2)
Supporting details: monitor is too close to the keyboard (Par. 5, line 3); keyboard is too small (Par. 5, lines 3–4); people use their laptops in bed, in the car, or on a train (Par. 5, lines 5–6)

long time

Answers will vary.

MAIN IDEA CHECK (page 179)

Paragraphs 1–4
A 3 **B** 1 **C** 2 **D** 4

Paragraphs 5–7
E 6 **F** 7 **G** 5

A CLOSER LOOK (page 180)

1 a (Par. 1, lines 15–16); c (Par. 1, lines 16–17); d (Par. 1, lines 14–15)
2 Answers will vary. Injuries include: strain on the eyes, neck, back, and shoulders.
3 (1) adjust chair height (Par. 4, lines 3–4); (2) use ergonomic keyboard (Par. 4, lines 10–11); (3) use a chair with back support (Par. 4, lines 7–8)
4 (1) a laptop's monitor is too close to the keyboard (Par. 5, line 3); (2) the keyboard is too small (Par. 5, lines 3–4); (3) people use them in bed, in a car, or on a train (Par. 5, lines 5–6)
5 c (Par. 6, lines 4–5)
6 a the correct height . . . with your head straight. (Par. 4, lines 4–5)
   b flat on the ground (Par. 4, line 7)
   c 11 billion dollars (Par. 6, line 5)
   d 1 million (Par. 6, line 6)

VOCABULARY STUDY: SYNONYMS (page 180)

1 slide **2** joints **3** muscles **4** repeated **5** arrangement **6** shoulders **7** height **8** parallel
9 lean **10** miss

VOCABULARY STUDY: WORD FAMILIES (page 181)

1 injured **2** adjustable **3** risky **4** injuries **5** adjust **6** strain **7** risked **8** correspondence
9 strain **10** corresponded

VOCABULARY REVIEW: SAME OR DIFFERENT (page 182)

1 S **2** S **3** D **4** S **5** D **6** S

SKILLS AND STRATEGIES 10 TAKING NOTES FROM A READING

SKILL PRACTICE 1 (page 184)

Answers will vary.

Before the invention of the sewing machine, clothes were made by hand one at a time. This took a long time. (Technology, however, has completely changed the manufacturing of clothes.) (1) In the 1830s, the sewing machine was invented. This changed the way clothes were made. Military uniforms were the first items of clothing to be produced using this technology. Production increased as technology continued to change. (2) In 1859, a foot pedal was added to the sewing machine. Now clothing could be made more quickly. (3) Later, after the invention of the electric sewing machine, clothing could easily be mass-produced. (4) More recently, computer technology has dramatically changed the design and the manufacture of clothes. (5) It now takes only ninety minutes for computers and automatic machines to make a man's suit. This is a huge savings in time and labor from the hard, slow work of sewing by hand.

invented: first made; military: army; suit: jacket and pants

SKILL PRACTICE 2 (pages 184–185)

I. Skirts – long history
   A. Ancient times
      1. Men and women wore skirts
      2. Skirts made of animal fur
   B. By eighteenth century
      1. Men no longer wore skirts
      2. Women's skirts were long + full – 2 meters across
   C. 1920s
      1. Coco Chanel raised skirts to knee
   D. Modern times
      1. 1960s – Mary Quant created miniskirts
      2. Late 1970s, miniskirts were no longer popular

SKILL PRACTICE 3 (page 185)

Answers will vary.

An interior designer is a person who designs the spaces where people work and live. (The demand for interior designers is growing in the United States; however, students should think carefully before choosing this career.) They need to understand what skills they must have. (1) First, an interior designer needs to have advanced computer skills because many companies use software programs for design. (2) Second, they need to understand the basics of engineering and art. (3) Good communication skills are also very important. Designers must clearly explain their ideas to their customers. (4) Finally, designers usually need a college degree. After they receive the degree, (5) they will need to work for about three years at a beginning level. During this time, the salary is not very high. (6) Students should also know that the number of interior designers is expected to grow at 19 percent for the next few years. It will soon be quite difficult to find design work because so many people are choosing interior design as a career.

advanced: high level

I. Interior designer – think before choosing career
   A. Skills needed
      1. Advanced computer skills
      2. Basics of engineering and art
      3. Good communication skills
      4. College degree

B. After college
    1. Work for 3 years – beginning level
    2. Low salary at this time
C. Number of interior designers – increase by 19%
    1. May be difficult to find job

READING 3   THE DESIGN OF LIVING SPACE

GETTING A FIRST IDEA ABOUT THE ARTICLE (page 186)

Answers will vary.

PARAGRAPH	QUESTION
2	How do we design balance?
3	What are some other examples of feng shui guidelines?
4	What colors have an emotional effect?
5	How can you make small homes more functional?
6	How does design help meet our basic needs?

WHILE YOU READ (pages 187–188)

balance
Feng shui: an Eastern philosophy (Par. 2, line 5); *Yin*: quiet, passive energy (Par. 2, lines 6–7);
Yang: strong and active energy (Par. 2, line 7)

room
Answers will vary.

Feng shui provides guidelines about how to decorate a room. In a bedroom, for example, the head of the bed should point in the correct direction. (1) It should point north for an older married couple. North is a quiet, peaceful direction. (2) For a young adult, however, feng shui says the head of the bed should point south. This direction has more energy and passion. (3) The head of the bed must not point northeast because this direction causes nightmares. (4) Also, a bedroom should not have any mirrors in it because mirrors make it difficult to get rid of negative energy.

direction: the position something faces; passion: very strong emotion

I. Feng shui – guidelines about bedroom
  A. Bed face north
    1. Quiet, peaceful direction
    2. Good for older people
  B. Bed face south
    1. Energy and passion
    2. Good for younger adults
  C. No mirrors
    1. Difficult to get rid of negative energy

interior design
Answers will vary.
I. Colors – different emotional and physical effects
  A. Red
    1. Most exciting – stimulating color
    2. Causes nightmares in bedrooms
  B. Green
    1. Peaceful
    2. Some cultures – good health and good luck
  C. Blue
    1. Peace and security

D. White
    1. Most used color
    2. Color of balance
    3. Makes small rooms look bigger and brighter (Par. 4)

portable
    can easily be moved (Par. 5, lines 10–11)

personalities
    Answers will vary.

MAIN IDEA CHECK (page 188)

A 5 **B** 3 **C** 1 **D** 6 **E** 4 **F** 2

A CLOSER LOOK (page 189)

1 c (Par. 1, lines 7–9)
2 False (Par. 2, lines 6–7)
3 Answers will vary. The head of the bed should point north (Par. 3, line 3); the bedroom should not have any mirrors. (Par. 3, lines 7–9)
4 b (Par. 4, lines 5–6); c (Par. 4, line 5); d (Par. 4, lines 7–8)
5 b
6 a (Par. 5, lines 8–11); c (Par. 3, lines 6–7)

VOCABULARY STUDY: SYNONYMS (page 190)

1 relax **2** reflect **3** stranger **4** combination **5** achieve **6** philosophy **7** guidelines **8** passion
9 dresser **10** majority

VOCABULARY STUDY: WORDS IN CONTEXT (page 190)

1 organized **2** got rid of **3** stimulating **4** personality **5** calm **6** negative **7** nightmares **8** balance
9 style **10** represents

READING 4 FASHION

GETTING A FIRST IDEA ABOUT THE ARTICLE (page 192)

SECTION	HEADING	TOPICS	✓
II	Fashion and Identity	A history of fashion	✓
		Fashion and personal identity	✓
		How clothes are made	
		Changes in women's fashion	✓
		Top designers in women's fashions	
III	How Fashion Moves Through Society	Factors in fashion trends	✓
		Tattoos as fashion	✓
		Where to study fashion	
		The role of designers in fashion trends	✓
		Fashion trends in Asia	
IV	Why Fashions Change	What is coming next in fashion	
		How young people affect fashion	✓
		The business of fashion	✓
		The science of fashion	

Fashion

Main idea: (They help us to express our personal identities . . . tell other people how we want them to see us.) (Par. 2, lines 3–5)

history

Answers will vary (Par. 3)

    Clothing design has described and defined us throughout history. In earlier times, clothing provided a lot of information about the people who wore the clothing. (It showed where they were from, their job, their social class, and sometimes even their religion.) Until the end of the nineteenth century, clothing continued to signal differences, especially in social class. (1) The working class wore clothes that were easy to move in; (2) they were designed for physical labor. (3) In contrast, the clothes of the elite often restricted movement; (4) they were designed for leisure. Their clothes sent a very clear message that the people wearing them did not do any hard work.

social class: economic background; physical labor: hard work; elite: a small group of very rich people

I. In the past, clothing identified people's jobs and origins
    A. Working class
        1. Easy to work in
        2. Designed for physical labor
    B. Elite
        1. Clothes restricted movement
        2. Sent message – elite don't do physical labor

change

Answers will vary.
I. Women's fashions changed
    A. World War I
        1. Women went to work
        2. Many began to wear pants
    B. Today
        1. Many still wear pants
        2. Short skirts, high heels are difficult to work in (Par. 5)

high-heeled shoes

Answers will vary.

shopping malls

a place where you can find many different kinds of stores together in one large area (Par. 6)

demand for this style

Main idea: (Top designers quickly noticed a demand for this style.) (Par. 8, line 7)
Examples: Snoop Dogg (Par. 8, line 4); LL Cool J and P. Diddy (Par. 8, line 7); Young people all over the world (Par. 8, lines 8–9)

generation

people who are about the same age in a family or society

will remain successful

Answers will vary.

MAIN IDEA CHECK (pages 196–197)

Paragraphs 1–5
A 3 **B** 5 **C** 2 **D** 4 **E** 1

Paragraphs 6–9
F 7 **G** 6 **H** 9 **I** 8

Paragraphs 10–12
J 10 **K** 12 **L** 11

A CLOSER LOOK (pages 197–198)

1 c (Par. 3)

2 restrictive clothing (Par. 3, line 8); long painted fingernails (Par. 4, lines 4–5); bound feet (Par. 4, lines 6–7); long, full dresses (Par. 5, line 5)

3 b (Par. 5, lines 1–4)

4 I. Top-down trend
   A. Until 20th century
     1. Middle class copied elite fashion
     2. Elite wore Paris-designed clothes
   B. Top-down trend still here today
     1. Armani, Ralph Lauren, and Koji Tatsuno
     2. Celebrities wear these clothes
   C. Demand increases
     1. Less famous designers produce similar but cheaper clothes
     2. Available in shopping malls for average person

5 **a** Versace, Hilfiger, Lauren (Par. 8, lines 1–3)
  b 1994 (Par. 8, lines 4–5)
  c 500 million U.S. dollars (Par. 8, lines 7–8)
  d sweatshirts, large pants, expensive sports shoes (Par. 8, lines 8–10)

6 C → A → E → B → D

7 False (Par. 9, lines 1–2)

8 B → A → D → C

9 Answers will vary.
   I. Clothing business depends on new demand
   A. People get rid of usable clothes
   B. Fashion business must persuade people to buy new clothes
     1. Change fashions all the time
     2. Examples: skirt length; height of heels; new colors

VOCABULARY STUDY: SYNONYMS (page 198)

1 jewelry **2** message **3** leisure **4** (to) bind **5** sweatshirts **6** uniform **7** military **8** prisons
9 tough **10** outsiders

VOCABULARY STUDY: WORD FAMILIES (page 199)

1 torn **2** appeal **3** adoption **4** restrictive **5** appeal **6** dominate **7** adopted **8** tear
9 restricted **10** domination

VOCABULARY REVIEW: SAME OR DIFFERENT (page 200)

1 S **2** D **3** S **4** S **5** D **6** S

MAKING CONNECTIONS

EXERCISE 1 (page 201)

1   (Objects) are often redesigned) in order to improve (their) usability. One example of (this) is wheeled luggage. (People) no longer strain joints and muscles because (they) don't have to lift heavy luggage.) (This) results in fewer injuries.

2 The New York Museum of Modern Art has a collection of everyday objects. A paper clip, a bottle opener, and a plastic top on a cup are examples of objects in the museum. These objects all provide simple solutions to everyday problems. Because (they) are functional and easy to use, (these objects) have become a part of everyday life.

3 (Interior designers) work in many different types of spaces. (Some) focus on one aspect of design, such as preventing repeated injuries with computers. (Others), however, design homes and create spaces that reflect the owners' personalities. A third group may design specific spaces, such as hotel rooms.

4 It is important to be comfortable when you are driving for a long time. Before you drive, you should adjust the seat to correspond to your height. You should also adjust your seat to lean backward a little bit. Finally, make sure the safety belt is flat over your shoulder.

5 Musicians have always influenced fashion design. For example, (Elvis Presley) dominated rock music in the late 1950s and early 1960s. (His) music and fashion reflected new ideas at that time and were very popular. Because of (his) popularity, young people adopted (his) style and wore "Elvis clothes."

EXERCISE 2 (page 202)
1 C, B, A
2 B, A, C
3 B, C, A
4 A, C, B
5 B, A, C

UNIT 6 The Brain and Behavior

SKILLS AND STRATEGIES 11 COLLOCATION

SKILL PRACTICE 1 (page 206)

1 to   **2** making   **3** pay, to   **4** play, in   **5** for

SKILL PRACTICE 2 (pages 206–207)

1 video games   **2** develop   **3** keep, of   **4** follow   **5** push   **6** at   **7** challenges   **8** take, of

SKILL PRACTICE 3 (page 207)

1 based on   **2** spent, years   **3** high standards   **4** depend on   **5** in a bad mood   **6** stay away from
7 taking risks

READING 1 BRAIN DEVELOPMENT AND FUNCTION

GETTING A FIRST IDEA ABOUT THE ARTICLE (page 208)

Answers will vary.

PARAGRAPH	QUESTION
1	What does the brain do?
3	How do different parts of the brain work?
4	When does the brain grow the fastest?
6	What things do we not know about the brain?

WHILE YOU READ (pages 209–211)

to it
consists of (Par. 2, line 1); high speeds (Par. 2, line 3); plays a role (Par. 2, line 14); responsible for (Par. 2, line 18); process information (Par. 2, line 20)

drove
forced something through something else (Par. 3)

much sense
Main idea: (Scientists have studied people with brain damage in order to understand how different parts of the brain work.) (Par. 3, lines 1–2)
Examples: (1) For example, . . . Phineas Gage . . . they discovered that a specific part of the brain controls personality and emotions (Par. 2, lines 2–4); (2) Scientists . . . by studying patients with brain damage (Par. 2, lines 8–10)

images
electronic pictures or photographs (Par. 5)

challenges of
developments in (Par. 6, line 2); suffer from (Par. 6, line 4); respond to (Par. 6, line 6)

MAIN IDEA CHECK (page 211)

A 6   **B** 1   **C** 5   **D** 4   **E** 3   **F** 2

A CLOSER LOOK (page 212)

1 a the cerebral cortex (Par. 2, lines 18–20)
  b the cerebellum (Par. 2, lines 10–11)
  c the brain stem (Par. 2, lines 7–8)
  d the cerebral cortex (Par. 2, lines 18–20)
2 False (Par. 2, lines 11–12)
3 c (Par. 3, lines 2–4)
4 b (Par. 4, lines 7–8)
5 False (Par. 4, lines 14–15)
6 a (Par. 5, lines 7–8)

VOCABULARY STUDY: SYNONYMS (page 213)

1 structure   **2** neurons   **3** resemble(s)   **4** speech   **5** patient   **6** behavior   **7** selfish   **8** impulsive
9 consistent   **10** surge

VOCABULARY STUDY: WORDS IN CONTEXT (page 213)

1 processed   **2** make sense   **3** suffers from   **4** back and forth   **5** keep track of   **6** nervous system
7 a great deal of   **8** involved in   **9** sensitive to   **10** consists of

READING 2   THE TEENAGE BRAIN

GETTING A FIRST IDEA ABOUT THE ARTICLE (page 215)

Answers will vary.
1 a
2 Teenage boys take risks.
3 She has an early class. She has stayed up late studying for a test. This is familiar to me. I have often had early classes, especially in high school. I stay up late the night before tests, and then feel very tired.

WHILE YOU READ (pages 216–218)

This difference
  Topic: (a teenage brain)
  Claim: is different from an adult brain (Par. 1, lines 10–11)

Studies of the brain
  good at (Par. 3, line 3); compared to (Par. 3, line 6); related to (Par. 3, line 10); angry at (Par. 3, line 14)

do not use good judgment
  (1) incomplete brain development (Par. 4, lines 7–8); (2) increase in hormones that affect behavior (Par. 4, lines 8–9)

positive
  Main idea: (Another factor . . . is lack of sleep.) (Par. 5, lines 1–2)
  Supporting details: stay up late (Par. 5, line 2); chemical is released later in teenagers (Par. 5, line 6); must get up early to go to school (Par. 5, line 8)

affect teenagers
  raised questions (Par. 6, lines 1–2); brought about changes (Par. 6, line 2); commit a crime (Par. 6, line 8); taking (new research) into account (Par. 6, lines 10–11)

MAIN IDEA CHECK (page 218)

A 3 **B** 2 **C** 6 **D** 4 **E** 1 **F** 5

A CLOSER LOOK (page 219)

1 (1) changes in hormone levels (Par. 1, lines 6–7); (2) difference between adult and teenage brain (Par. 1, lines 10–11)
2 a, c, d (Par. 2, lines 5–8)
3 b (Par. 3, lines 9–12)
4 True (Par. 4, lines 8–11)
5 b (Par. 5, lines 5–8)
6 (1) schools are starting the school day later (Par. 6, lines 3–4); (2) offer difficult classes later in the day (Par. 6, lines 5–6); (3) the legal system is considering the types of penalties for adolescents (Par. 6, lines 10–11)

VOCABULARY STUDY: SYNONYMS (page 219)

1 adolescence **2** notice(d) **3** hormone **4** spatial **5** upset **6** examine(d) **7** crucial **8** lack
9 stay up **10** officials

VOCABULARY STUDY: WORD FAMILIES (page 220)

1 released **2** stressful **3** explored **4** independence **5** judgment **6** stress **7** independent **8** release
9 exploration **10** judge

VOCABULARY REVIEW: SAME OR DIFFERENT (page 221)

1 S **2** D **3** D **4** S **5** S **6** S

SKILLS AND STRATEGIES 12 PREPARING FOR A READING TEST

SKILL PRACTICE 1 (page 223)

Answers will vary.
1 A neurologist is a scientist who studies the brain.
2 Images of brain activity identify which parts of the brain are responsible for which activity.
3 The frontal lobes are responsible.

SKILL PRACTICE 2 (page 224)

Answers will vary.
1 What are the two halves of the brain called?
2 What does each side do?
3 What is one characteristic of a right-brain thinker?

SKILL PRACTICE 3 (page 224)

Answers will vary.

The brain is the most complex machine in existence. (1) It weighs only about 1.5 kilograms, but it is much more complicated than the most powerful computer. (2) It has over 100 billion neurons. These neurons send messages across synapses, which are like a wire connecting two battery cells. (3) Each neuron has as many as 10,000 synapses. If every person in the world made a phone call at the same time, that would equal the same number of connections that a single brain makes in a day. (4) Neurons send messages at speeds of over 300 kilometers per hour. If these cells become damaged by disease or accident, they may not grow back again. Today's scientists know a great deal about the human brain, but they also know that they still have much more to learn about this very complex organ.

complex: very complicated; neurons: cells that send messages to the brain; synapses: connections between neurons that carry messages

Possible questions and answers:
1 What do neurons do? They send messages across synapses.
2 What are synapses? They are like wires that connect neurons.
3 How many synapses does each neuron have? They have about 10,000.
4 How fast can the brain send messages? They can travel 300 km per hour.
5 If brain cells are damaged, do they always grow back? No.

READING 3 THE MALE AND FEMALE BRAIN

GETTING A FIRST IDEA ABOUT THE ARTICLE (page 225)

PARAGRAPH	STATEMENT	T / F
1	In the past, people believed male and female brains were different.	T
2	Men have stronger verbal abilities than women.	F
3	As boys and girls grow older, their brains continue to be different.	T
4	Men and women have the same abilities.	F
5	Men and women think about information differently.	T
6	Women's intuition is the ability to focus on the details.	F
7	Scientists cannot explain why male and female brains developed differently.	F
8	All men have some abilities that are also typical of women.	F

WHILE YOU READ (pages 226–228)

more important, role
Answers will vary.
Why do men and women have different abilities? (Par. 1)

continue
Boys' behavior: remembered objects (Par. 3, lines 4–5); more likely to be interested in toys such as trucks (Par. 3, lines 6–7); tend to play and fight physically (Par. 3, lines 8–9)
Girls' behavior: remembered people (Par. 3, lines 3–4); more likely to be interested in toys that look like people (Par. 3, lines 7–8); play more quietly (Par. 3, line 9); solve their problems with words (Par. 3, lines 9–10)

plan
tasks that require spatial ability (Par. 4, line 2)

information
Answers will vary.
Explain how men and women think about information differently.

develop
Main idea: Therefore, . . . different parts of their brains developed to perform these responsibilities.
(Par. 7, lines 4–5)
Supporting details:
(1) For example . . . differences in spatial abilities . . . men were hunters. (Par. 7, lines 5–7)
(2) Their superior physical coordination . . . advantage in hunting. (Par. 7, lines 7–8)
(3) They remembered . . . nearby landmarks. (Par. 7, lines 11–12)
(4) Women . . . understanding feelings was an important part of this activity. (Par. 7, lines 12–13)

MAIN IDEA CHECK (pages 228–229)

Paragraphs 1–4
A 2 **B** 1 **C** 4 **D** 3

Paragraphs 5–8
E 8 **F** 7 **G** 5 **H** 6

A CLOSER LOOK (page 229)

1 False (Par. 1, lines 6–9)

2 Answers will vary.
  I. Women – stronger verbal abilities than men
    A. Female brain
      1. Uses left and right hemisphere
      2. Has wider corpus callosum
    B. Male brain
      1. Uses mainly the left hemisphere
    C. Results: women understand + respond more quickly (Par. 2)

3 Answers will vary.

GIRLS	BOYS
remember faces (Par. 3, lines 3–4)	remember objects (Par. 3, lines 4–5)
play with dolls (Par. 3, lines 7–8)	play with trucks and building toys (Par. 3, lines 6–7)
play quietly (Par. 3, line 9)	play / fight physically (Par. 3, lines 8–9)
solve problems with words (Par. 3, lines 9–10)	

4 Men are better than women at tasks that require spatial ability. (Par. 4, lines 1–2)

5 b (Par. 5, lines 4–5); c (Par. 6, lines 2–3); e (Par. 6, lines 7–9)

6 Answers will vary. Women understood feelings, which was part of raising children (Par. 7, lines 12–13); men used physical coordination for hunting. (Par. 7, lines 8–9)

7 True (Par. 8)

VOCABULARY STUDY: SYNONYMS (page 230)

1 biology **2** verbal **3** (to) recall **4** tend to **5** imagine **6** route **7** intuition **8** interpret **9** hunters
10 superior

VOCABULARY STUDY: WORDS IN CONTEXT (page 230)

1 raising children **2** landmark **3** three-dimensional **4** coordination **5** collecting **6** conducted
7 sensed **8** distinct **9** made up of **10** extensive

READING 4 ADDICTION AND THE BRAIN

GETTING A FIRST IDEA ABOUT THE ARTICLE (page 232)

Answers will vary.

SECTION	HEADING	QUESTION
II	The Role of Pleasure in Addiction	1. What is dopamine? 2. Why do people become addicted to playing video games?
III	Stopping an Addiction	1. Why can't an addict just stop that behavior? 2. What role does the environment play in addiction?
IV	Treatment	1. How do professionals help addicts end an addiction? 2. Why is it important for addicts to change their behavior?

brain

Answers will vary.

breakthrough: important discovery (Par. 2, line 2); dopamine: neurotransmitter (Par. 2, lines 3–4)

behavior

Main idea: Dopamine is connected to survival. (Par. 6, line 3)

Supporting details:

(1) For example, when you eat . . . feeling of pleasure. (Par. 6, lines 3–4)

(2) The brain remembers . . . connects it to the activity of eating. (Par. 6, lines 5–6)

(3) In this way . . . in order to survive. (Par. 6, lines 6–7)

(4) Drugs imitate the same process. (Par. 6, line 7)

(5) The brain . . . continue the activity. (Par. 6, lines 7–8)

well

Answers will vary.

1. What happens when you are very frightened?

2. Why does the part of the brain controlling judgment shut down when you are in danger? (Par. 7)

addiction

I. Stress increases the chance that people will become addicts.

  A. Happy rats

    1. Lots of food, friends, and space

    2. Did not take water with addictive drug

  B. Stressed rats

    1. Left alone, small cage

    2. Took water with addictive drug (Par. 9)

Addicts usually

take medicine (Par. 10, line 2); prevent diseases (Par. 10, line 4); solve the problem (Par. 10, line 8)

life again

Answers will vary.

1. What is a vaccine?

2. Why should addicts keep away from some people?

MAIN IDEA CHECK (pages 236)

Paragraphs 1–5

A 2 **B** 3 **C** 4 **D** 1 **E** 5

Paragraphs 6–9

F 8 **G** 9 **H** 7 **I** 6

Paragraphs 10–12

J 11 **K** 13 **L** 10 **M** 12

A CLOSER LOOK (pages 237–238)

1 c (Par. 1, lines 6–7); e (Par. 1, lines 7–8)

2 C → E → A → B → D

3 False (Par. 4, lines 4–6); (Par. 5, lines 2–3)

4 a (Par. 7, lines 6–9)

5 b (Par. 9, lines 2–4)

6 True (Par. 9, lines 2–3)

7 b (Par. 10, lines 6–7)

8 (1) admit they have a problem (Par. 11, lines 2–3); (2) stay away from people and places connected to the addiction (Par. 11, lines 3–5)

9 I. Difficult to stop an addiction to an activity
  A. Young children
    1. Feel angry if activity is taken away
    2. Slowly reduce time spent on activity

VOCABULARY STUDY: SYNONYMS (page 238)

1 attitude **2** breakthrough **3** nicotine **4** flood(s) **5** used to **6** desire **7** purchase **8** imitate
9 vaccine **10** antibodies

VOCABULARY STUDY: WORD FAMILIES (pages 238–239)

1 treat **2** clarify **3** interruptions **4** treatment **5** threatened **6** anxiety **7** threat **8** interrupted
9 clear **10** anxious

VOCABULARY REVIEW: SAME OR DIFFERENT (page 239)

1 D **2** S **3** S **4** D **5** D **6** D

MAKING CONNECTIONS

EXERCISE 1 (page 241)

1   Some people suffer from loss of memory as they get older. Usually, they lose their most recent memories first. Gradually, they forget other things, including where they live. This memory loss can lead to a great deal of stress for the people who love and take care of them.

2   There are several distinct types of memory. One type is known as short-term memory. Researchers have conducted experiments to understand more about short-term memory. They have found that short-term memory only lasts for about thirty seconds.

3   Humans have very good vision compared to many animals. Some animals do not have good vision, but their other senses are powerful. For example, cats have an excellent sense of smell and hearing. In contrast, some insects cannot hear, but they are sensitive to movement.

4   An atlas is usually a book of maps, but scientists are working on a new kind of atlas – an atlas of the brain. This atlas consists of images of seven thousand healthy brains. The scientists plan to put these images on the Internet so that people can see them in three dimensions. The images will help future scientists understand more about the brain.

5   Several studies have explored the idea that music can improve intelligence. One study claimed that music lessons could improve spatial processing. Another study tried to show that music lessons improve memory. However, no studies have shown a consistent effect of music on intelligence.

EXERCISE 2 (page 242)

1 B, A, C
2 C, B, A
3 C, B, A
4 A, C, B
5 C, A, B